GLSL Essentials

Enrich your 3D scenes with the power of GLSL!

Jacobo Rodríguez

PUBLISHING

BIRMINGHAM - MUMBAI

GLSL Essentials

First published: December 2013

Production Reference: 1181213

Published by Packt Publishing Ltd.
Livery Place
35 Livery Street
Birmingham B3 2PB, UK.

ISBN 978-1-84969-800-9

www.packtpub.com

Cover Image by Jacobo Rodríguez Villar (jrodriguez@parallel-games.com)

Credits

Author

Jacobo Rodríguez

Reviewers

Dimitrios Christopoulos

Toni Ascó González

Oscar Ripolles

Acquisition Editors

Antony Lowe

Rebecca Pedley

Commissioning Editors

Subho Gupta

Priyanka Shah

Sharvari Tawde

Technical Editors

Venu Manthena

Gaurav Thingalaya

Project Coordinator

Amey Sawant

Proofreaders

Maria Gould

Paul Hindle

Indexer

Priya Subramani

Graphics

Ronak Dhruv

Production Coordinator

Shantanu Zagade

Cover Work

Shantanu Zagade

About the Author

Jacobo Rodríguez is a real-time computer graphics programmer living in the north of Spain. He has working experience with computer graphics, digital photogrammetry, computer vision, and video game development. Jacobo has worked for cutting-edge technology companies such as Metria Digital and Blit Software, and has also worked as an entrepreneur and freelancer for a variety of clients of platforms such as PC, iOS, PlayStation 3, PlayStation Vita, and PlayStation Portable. Jacobo has been working and learning at the same time for the last 20 years in the computer graphics field in roles ranging from junior programmer to project manager, passing through R&D director as well. Jacobo has always been very committed to the computer graphics community, having released for free the OpenGL Shader Designer: the first application in the world (even before NVIDIA with FX Composer or ATI with RenderMonkey) designed to visually develop and program GLSL shaders, as well as some OpenGL programming tutorials, all forming part of the Official OpenGL SDK.

I would like to thank my family for supporting me in those late nights and weekend writing sessions. I would also like to thank Toni Ascó Emilio, José Dominguez, and Iñaki Griego, for their invaluable support and resources during the production of this book.

About the Reviewers

Dimitrios Christopoulos studied Computer Engineering and Informatics and holds a Master of Science degree in Virtual Reality and Computer Graphics. He has 16+ years of experience in 3D computer graphics with a strong specialty in C/C++/OpenGL and Linux. Dimi has worked for European Union research projects, Indie game productions, and museums producing games, educational applications, and cultural heritage productions for desktops and virtual reality installations such as Domes, Caves, Reality Centers, and Powerwalls. His research interests include virtual reality, human computer interaction, computer graphics, and games, with numerous publications in relevant conferences and journals. Dimitrios has been an author of the book *More OpenGL Programming*, *Course Technology PTR*, and has contributed to *OpenGL Programming*, *Prima Tech*, and has been a reviewer for *OpenGL Development Cookbook*, *Packt Publishing*.

I would like to thank my wife Giota for being supportive during my late night reviewing sessions.

Toni Ascó González holds a Master's degree in Computer Science specializing in real-time graphics and OpenGL. For the past 16 years, he has been programming graphics applications from virtual reality to video games. He founded a virtual reality company in Barcelona, and dedicated eight years to develop a state-of-the-art, real-time software for architectural visualization. After that experience, he moved to Bravo Game Studios and developed video games for mobile platforms and portable consoles. Currently, he applies his experience in 3D and real-time graphics in the virtual gambling field.

I would like to thank my other half, Chu, for her patience, love, and care. Life would be uninteresting and void without you at my side. Of course, thanks to my mother and my brother for being my foundation and supporting my love for computers since I was nine. I would also like to thank all of the mentors and colleagues who have been with me over all these years. Bernat Muñoz, Alex Novell, and Marc Martí from Insideo for all those wonderful years experimenting with new techniques. Also, Alberto García-Baquero, Benjamín de la Fuente, and Miguel Guillén, who have shown me new and amazing ways of doing things, and given me new perspectives on product development. Finally, a special mention to Jacobo Rodriguez Villar; without him, I wouldn't be where I am.

Oscar Ripolles received his degree in Computer Engineering in 2004 and his Ph.D. in 2009 at the Universitat Jaume I in Castellon (Spain). He has also been a researcher at the Université de Limoges (France) and at the Universidad Politecnica de Valencia (Spain). He is currently woking in neuroimaging at Neuroelectrics in Barcelona (Spain). His research interests include multiresolution modeling, geometry optimization, hardware programming, and medical imaging.

www.PacktPub.com

Support files, eBooks, discount offers and more

You might want to visit www.PacktPub.com for support files and downloads related to your book.

Did you know that Packt offers eBook versions of every book published, with PDF and ePub files available? You can upgrade to the eBook version at www.PacktPub.com and as a print book customer, you are entitled to a discount on the eBook copy. Get in touch with us at service@packtpub.com for more details.

At www.PacktPub.com, you can also read a collection of free technical articles, sign up for a range of free newsletters and receive exclusive discounts and offers on Packt books and eBooks.

http://PacktLib.PacktPub.com

Do you need instant solutions to your IT questions? PacktLib is Packt's online digital book library. Here, you can access, read and search across Packt's entire library of books.

Why Subscribe?

- Fully searchable across every book published by Packt
- Copy and paste, print and bookmark content
- On demand and accessible via web browser

Free Access for Packt account holders

If you have an account with Packt at www.PacktPub.com, you can use this to access PacktLib today and view nine entirely free books. Simply use your login credentials for immediate access.

Table of Contents

Preface   **1**

Chapter 1: The Graphics Rendering Pipeline   **5**

A brief history of graphics hardware   **6**
The Graphics Rendering Pipeline   **8**
   Geometry stages (per-vertex operations)   8
   Fragment stages (per-fragment operations)   9
   External stages   10
   Differences between fixed and programmable designs   10
Types of shaders   **11**
   Vertex shaders   12
   Fragment shaders   12
   Geometry shaders   13
   Compute shaders   13
GPU, a vectorial and parallel architecture   **14**
The shader environment   **15**
Summary   **16**

Chapter 2: GLSL Basics   **17**

The Language   **17**
Language basics   **18**
   Instructions   18
   Basic types   19
   Variable initializers   20
   Vector and matrix operations   22
   Castings and conversions   23
   Code comments   23
   Flow control   23
   Loops   26
   Structures   27

Arrays	28
Functions	29
Preprocessor	32
Shader input and output variables	**35**
Uniform variables	35
Other input variables	36
Shader output variables	37
Summary	**38**
Chapter 3: Vertex Shaders	**39**
Vertex shader inputs	**39**
Vertex attributes	40
Uniform variables	42
Vertex shader outputs	**43**
Drawing a simple geometry sample	**44**
Distorting a geometry sample	46
Using interpolators	48
Simple lighting	50
Basic lighting theory	50
Lighting example code	52
Summary	**55**
Chapter 4: Fragment Shaders	**57**
Execution model	**57**
Terminating a fragment shader	58
Inputs and outputs	**58**
Examples	**60**
Solid color mesh	60
Interpolated colored mesh	61
Using interpolators to compute the texture coordinates	62
Phong lighting	63
Summary	**69**
Chapter 5: Geometry Shaders	**71**
Geometry shaders versus vertex shaders	**71**
Inputs and outputs	**72**
Interface blocks	73
Example – pass-thru shader	75
Example – using attributes in the interface blocks	76
A crowd of butterflies	78
Summary	**85**

Chapter 6: Compute Shaders   87
  Execution model   87
  Render to texture example   89
  Raw data computations   92
  Summary   95
Index   97

Preface

If you are still in the old fixed pipeline days and your OpenGL knowledge is a little bit rusty, or if you want to jump from OpenGL | ES to a more complete and modern version of OpenGL, then this book is for you. Inside the pages of this book, you will find the details of the most recent OpenGL Shading Language Version: 4.3.

This book has been written looking forward in the OpenGL specification. No old functionalities or deprecated code will be found in this book, just the plain 4.3 Version.

What this book covers

Chapter 1, *The Graphics Rendering Pipeline*, starts with a brief introduction to the rendering pipeline and moves on to give an overview of the programmable stages.

Chapter 2, *GLSL Basics*, covers language basics, types, vector operations, flow control, preprocessor, and shader inputs and outputs.

Chapter 3, *Vertex Shaders*, looks at the vertex programmable stage, uniform variables and basic lighting, and vertex shader examples.

Chapter 4, *Fragment Shaders*, looks at the execution model, inputs and outputs, and examples.

Chapter 5, *Geometry Shaders*, looks at geometry shader structure, interface blocks, and examples.

Chapter 6, *Compute Shaders*, covers the execution model, GPGPU basics, render to texture, and basic raw computations.

What you need for this book

In order to run the samples from this book, you will need a text editor and a C/C++ compiler. For the text editor, a free editor such as Notepad++ or SciTE could be used, and for the C/C++ compiler, GCC/G++, or Visual Studio (the Express version is free) are the best choices. As we are addressing the latest OpenGL version, a graphics card that supports at least OpenGL 4.3 will be needed.

Who this book is for

This book is for people who have some experience or basic knowledge in computer graphics and who want to upgrade their knowledge to the latest OpenGL version. It is also for people who want to take the jump from the fixed pipeline to the programmable pipeline.

Conventions

In this book, you will find a number of styles of text that distinguish between different kinds of information. Here are some examples of these styles, and an explanation of their meaning.

Code words in text, database table names, folder names, filenames, file extensions, pathnames, dummy URLs, user input, and Twitter handles are shown as follows: "The `buffer` keyword denotes the type of the interface block."

A block of code is set as follows:

```
layout(std430, binding = 0) buffer InputBufferA{float inA[];};
layout(std430, binding = 1) buffer InputBufferB{float inB[];};
layout(std430, binding=2) buffer OutputBuffer{float outBuffer[];};
```

When we wish to draw your attention to a particular part of a code block, the relevant lines or items are set in bold:

```
layout(std430, binding = 0) buffer InputBufferA{float inA[];};
layout(std430, binding = 1) buffer InputBufferB{float inB[];};
layout(std430, binding=2) buffer OutputBuffer{float outBuffer[];};
```

New terms and **important words** are shown in bold.

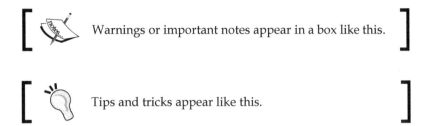

Warnings or important notes appear in a box like this.

Tips and tricks appear like this.

Reader feedback

Feedback from our readers is always welcome. Let us know what you think about this book—what you liked or may have disliked. Reader feedback is important for us to develop titles that you really get the most out of.

To send us general feedback, simply send an e-mail to feedback@packtpub.com, and mention the book title via the subject of your message. If there is a topic that you have expertise in and you are interested in either writing or contributing to a book, see our author guide on www.packtpub.com/authors.

Customer support

Now that you are the proud owner of a Packt book, we have a number of things to help you to get the most from your purchase.

Downloading the color images of this book

We also provide you a PDF file that has color images of the screenshots/diagrams used in this book. The color images will help you better understand the changes in the output. You can download this file from: http://www.packtpub.com/sites/default/files/downloads/8009ot_graphics.pdf.

Errata

Although we have taken every care to ensure the accuracy of our content, mistakes do happen. If you find a mistake in one of our books—maybe a mistake in the text or the code—we would be grateful if you would report this to us. By doing so, you can save other readers from frustration and help us improve subsequent versions of this book. If you find any errata, please report them by visiting http://www.packtpub.com/submit-errata, selecting your book, clicking on the **errata submission form** link, and entering the details of your errata. Once your errata are verified, your submission will be accepted and the errata will be uploaded on our website, or added to any list of existing errata, under the Errata section of that title. Any existing errata can be viewed by selecting your title from http://www.packtpub.com/support.

Piracy

Piracy of copyright material on the Internet is an ongoing problem across all media. At Packt, we take the protection of our copyright and licenses very seriously. If you come across any illegal copies of our works, in any form, on the Internet, please provide us with the location address or website name immediately so that we can pursue a remedy.

Please contact us at copyright@packtpub.com with a link to the suspected pirated material.

We appreciate your help in protecting our authors, and our ability to bring you valuable content.

Questions

You can contact us at questions@packtpub.com if you are having a problem with any aspect of the book, and we will do our best to address it.

1
The Graphics Rendering Pipeline

If this is your first approach to shader technology, you should know a few things before we start writing GLSL code. The differences between the usual CPU architecture and a GPU are big enough to warrant mentioning them.

When you programmed applications in the past, you were aware of the underlying hardware: it has a CPU, an ALU, and memory (both volatile or for massive storage) and certain types of I/O devices (keyboard, screen, and so on). You also knew that your program would run sequentially, one instruction after another (unless you use multithreading, but that is not the point). When programming shaders, they will be running in an isolated unit called GPU, which has a very different architecture than the one you are used to.

Now, your application will run in a massive parallel environment. The I/O devices are totally different; you won't have direct access of any kind of memory, nor will it be generic for you to use at your will. Also, the system will spawn your program in tens or hundreds of instances, as if they were running using hundreds of real hardware threads.

In order to understand this fairly new architecture, this chapter will cover the following topics:

- A brief history of graphics hardware
- The Graphics Rendering Pipeline
- Types of shaders
- The shader environment
- Scalar versus vectorial execution
- Parallel execution

A brief history of graphics hardware

Graphics hardware (also called a graphics card or GPU) is not only a bunch of transistors that receive some generic orders and input data; it acts consequently like a CPU does. Orders issued to the hardware must be consistent and have an explicit and well known order at every stage. There are also data requirements in order to make things work as expected (for example, you cannot use vertices as input for fragment shaders, or textures as output in geometry shaders). Data and orders must follow a path and have to pass through some stages, and that cannot be altered.

This path is commonly called **The Graphics Rendering Pipeline**. Think of it like a pipe where we insert some data into one end — vertices, textures, shaders — and they start to travel through some small machines that perform very precise and concrete operations on the data and produce the final output at the other end: the final rendering.

In the early OpenGL years, the Graphics Rendering Pipeline was completely fixed, which means that the data always had to go through the same small machines, that always did the same operations, in the same order, and no operation could be skipped. These were the pre-shader ages (2002 and earlier).

The following is a simplified representation of the fixed pipeline, showing the most important building blocks and how the data flows through:

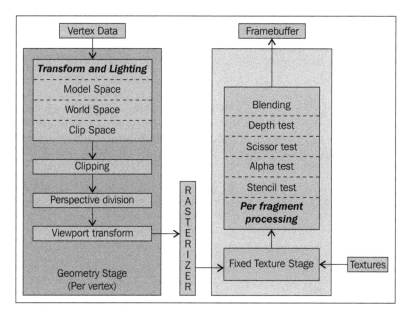

Between the years 2002 and 2004, some kind of programmability inside the GPU was made available, replacing some of those fixed stages. Those were the first shaders that graphics programmers had to code in a pseudo assembler language, and were very platform specific. In fact, programmers had to code at least one shader variant for each graphics hardware vendor, because they didn't share even the same assembler language, but at least they were able to replace some of the old-fashioned fixed pipeline stages by small low-level programs. Nonetheless, this was the beginning of the biggest revolution in real-time graphics programming history.

Some companies provided the programmers with other high-level programming solutions, such as Cg (from NVidia) or HLSL (from Microsoft), but those solutions weren't multiplatform. Cg was only usable with NVidia GPUs and HLSL was part of Direct3D.

During the year 2004, some companies realized the need for a high-level shader language, which would be common for different platforms; something like a standard for shader programming. Hence, **OpenGL Shading Language (GLSL)** was born and it allowed programmers to replace their multiple assembler code paths by a unique (at least in theory, because different GPUs have different capabilities) C-like shader, common for every hardware vendor.

In that year, only two pieces of the fixed pipeline could be replaced: the **vertex processing unit**, which took care of transform and lighting (T&L), and the **fragment processing unit** which was responsible for assigning colors to pixels. Those new programmable units were called **vertex shaders** and **fragment shaders** respectively. Also, another two stages were added later; geometry shaders and compute shaders were added to the official OpenGL specification in 2008 and 2012 respectively.

The following diagram shows an aspect of the new programmable pipeline after programmability changes:

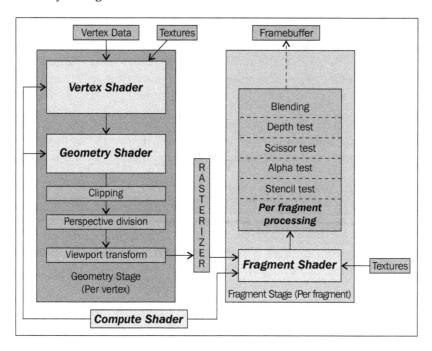

The Graphics Rendering Pipeline

In accordance with the programmable pipeline diagram, I'll describe, in a summarized way, the module that the data goes through to explain how it is transformed in every stage.

Geometry stages (per-vertex operations)

This block of stages focuses on the transformation of vertex data from its initial state (model coordinates system) to its final state (viewport coordinates system):

- **Vertex data**: This is the input data for the whole process. Here we feed the pipeline with all the vectorial data of our geometry: vertices, normals, indices, tangents, binormals, texture coordinates, and so on.

- **Textures**: When shaders showed up, this new input for the vertex stage was possible. In addition to making our renders colorful, textures might serve as an input in vertex and geometry shaders, to, for example, displace vertices according with the values stored into a texture (displacement mapping technique).

- **Vertex shader**: This system is responsible for the transformation of the vertices from their local coordinate system to the clip space, applying the adequate transform matrices (model, view, and projection).

- **Geometry shader**: New primitives could be generated using this module, with the outcome of the vertex shader as input.

- **Clipping**: Once the primitive's vertices are in the so-called clipping space, it is easier and computationally cheaper to clip and discard the outer triangles here rather than in any other space.

- **Perspective division**: This operation converts our visualization volume (a truncated pyramid, usually called a frustum) into a regular and normalized cube.

- **Viewport transform**: The near plane of the clipping volume (the normalized cube) is translated and scaled to the viewport coordinates. This means that the coordinates will be mapped to our viewport (usually our screen or our window).

- **Data is passed to the rasterizer**: This is the stage that transforms our vectorial data (the primitive's vertices) to a discrete representation (the framebuffer) to be processed in further steps.

Fragment stages (per-fragment operations)

Here is where our vectorial data is transformed into discrete data, ready to be rasterized. The stages inside the superblock controls show that discrete data will finally be presented:

- **Fragment shader**: This is the stage where texture, colors, and lights are calculated, applied, and combined to form a fragment.

- **Post fragment processing**: This is the stage where blending, depth tests, scissor tests, alpha tests, and so on take place. Fragments are combined, tested, and discarded in this stage and the ones that finally pass, are written to the framebuffer.

External stages

Outside the per-vertex and per-fragment big blocks lies the compute shader stage. This stage can be written to affect any other programmable part of the pipeline.

Differences between fixed and programmable designs

It is worth understanding the fixed pipeline, because the programmable pipeline is heavily based on it. Shaders only replace a few well defined modules that previously existed in a fixed way, so the concept of a "pipeline" has not actually changed very much.

In the case of the vertex shaders, they replace the whole transform and lighting module. Now we have to write a program that can perform equivalent tasks. Inside your vertex shader, you can perform the calculations that you would need for your purposes, but there is a minimum requirement. In order not to break the pipeline, the output of your shader must feed the input of the next module. You can achieve this by calculating the vertex position in clipping coordinates and writing it out for the next stage.

Regarding fragment shaders, they replace the fixed texture stages. In the past, this module cared about how a fragment was produced by combining textures in a very limited way. Currently, the final outcome of a fragment shader is a fragment. As implicitly said before, a fragment is a candidate to a pixel, so, in its most simple form, it is simply an RGBA color. To connect the fragment shader with the following pipeline's modules, you have to output that color, but you can compute it the way you want.

When your fragment shader produces a color, other data is also associated to it, mainly its raster position and depth, so further tests such as depth or scissor tests could go straight on. After all the fragments for a current raster position are processed, the color that remains is what is commonly called a pixel.

Optionally, you can specify two additional modules that did not exist in the fixed pipeline before:

- **The geometry shader**: This module is placed after the vertex shader, but before clipping happens. The responsibility of this module is to emit new primitives (not vertices!) based on the incoming ones.

- **The compute shader**: This is a complementary module. In some way, this is quite different to the other shaders because it affects the whole pipeline globally. Its main purpose is to provide a method for generic GPGPU (General-Purpose computation on GPUs); not very graphics related. It is like OpenCL, but more handy for graphics programmers because it is fully integrated with the entire pipeline. As graphic usage examples, they could be used for image transforms or for deferred rendering in a more efficient way than OpenCL.

Types of shaders

Vertex and fragment shaders are the most important shaders in the whole pipeline, because they expose the pure basic functionality of the GPU. With vertex shaders, you can compute the geometry of the object that you are going to render as well as other important elements, such as the scene's camera, the projection, or how the geometry is clipped. With fragment shaders, you can control how your geometry will look onscreen: colors, lighting, textures, and so on.

As you can see, with only vertex and fragment shaders, you can control almost everything in your rendering process, but there is room for more improvement in the OpenGL machine.

Let's put an example: suppose that you process point **primitives** with a complex vertex shader. Using those processed vertices, you can use a geometry shader to create arbitrary shaped primitives (for instance, quads) using the points as the quad's center. Then you can use those quads for a particle system.

During that process you have saved bandwidth, because you have sent points instead of quads that have four times more vertices and processing power because, once you have transformed the points, the other four vertices already lie in the same space, so you transformed one vertex with a complex shader instead of four.

Unlike vertex and fragment shaders (it is mandatory to have one of each kind to complete the pipeline) the geometry shader is only optional. So, if you do not want to create a new geometry after the vertex shader execution, simply do not link a geometry shader in your application, and the results of the vertex shader will pass unchanged to the clipping stage, which is perfectly fine.

The compute shader stage was the latest addition to the pipeline. It is also optional, like the geometry shader, and is intended for generic computations.

Inside the pipeline, some of the following shaders can exist: vertex shaders, fragment shaders, geometry shaders, tessellation shaders (meant to subdivide triangle meshes on the fly, but we are not covering them in this book), and compute shaders. OpenGL evolves every day, so don't be surprised if other shader classes appear and change the pipeline layout from time to time.

Before going deeper into the matter, there is an important concept that we have to speak about; the concept of a shader program. A shader program is nothing more than a working pipeline configuration. This means that at least a vertex shader and a fragment shader must have been compiled without errors, and linked together. As for geometry and compute shaders, they could form part of a program too, being compiled and linked together with the other two shaders into the same shader program.

Vertex shaders

In order to take your 3D model's coordinates and transform them to the clip space, we usually apply the model, view, and projection matrices to the vertices. Also, we can perform any other type of data transform, such as apply noise (from a texture or computed on the fly) to the positions for a pseudorandom displacement, calculate normals, calculate texture coordinates, calculate vertex colors, prepare the data for a normal mapping shader, and so on.

You can do a lot more with this shader; however, the most important aspect of it is to provide the vertex positions to clip coordinates, to take us to the next stage.

A vertex shader is a piece of code that is executed in the GPU processors, and it's executed once, and only once for each vertex you send to the graphics card. So, if you have a 3D model with 1000 vertices, the vertex shader will be executed 1000 times, so remember to keep your calculations always simple.

Fragment shaders

Fragment shaders are responsible for painting each primitive's area. The minimum task for a fragment shader is to output an RGBA color. You can calculate that color by any means: procedurally, from textures, or using vertex shader's output data. But in the end, you have to output at least a color to the framebuffer.

The execution model of a fragment shader is like the vertex shader's one. A fragment shader is a piece of code that is executed once, and only once, per fragment. Let us elaborate on this a bit. Suppose that you have a screen with a size of 1.024 x 768. That screen contains 786.432 pixels. Now suppose you paint one quad that covers exactly the whole screen (also known as a full screen quad). This means that your fragment shader will be executed 786.432 times, but the reality is worse. What if you paint several full screen quads (something normal when doing post-processing shaders such as motion blur, glows, or screen space ambient occlusion), or simply many triangles that overlap on the screen? Each time you paint a triangle on the screen, all its area must be rasterized, so all the triangle's fragments must be calculated. In reality, a fragment shader is executed millions of times. Optimization in a fragment shader is more critical than in the vertex shaders.

Geometry shaders

The geometry shader's stage is responsible for the creation of new rendering primitives parting from the output of the vertex shader. A geometry shader is executed once per primitive, which is, in the worst case (when it is used to emit point primitives), the same as the vertex shader. The best case scenario is when it is used to emit triangles, because only then will it be executed three times less than the vertex shader, but this complexity is relative. Although the geometry shader's execution could be cheap, it always increases the scene's complexity, and that always translates into more computational time spent by the GPU to render the scene.

Compute shaders

This special kind of shader does not relate directly to a particular part of the pipeline. They can be written to affect vertex, fragment, or geometry shaders.

As compute shaders lie in some manner outside the pipeline, they do not have the same constraints as the other kind of shaders. This makes them ideal for generic computations. Compute shaders are less specific, but have the advantage of having access to all functions (`matrix`, `advanced texture` functions, and so on) and data types (`vectors`, `matrices`, all texture formats, and `vertex buffers`) that exist in GLSL, while other GPGPU solutions, such as OpenCL or CUDA have their own specific data types and do not fit easily with the rendering pipeline.

GPU, a vectorial and parallel architecture

GPUs provide an incredible processing power in certain situations. If you ever tried to program a software rasterizer for your CPU, you would have noticed that the performance was terrible. Even the most advanced software rasterizer, taking advantage of vectorial instruction sets such as SSE3, or making intensive use of all available cores through multithreading, offers very poor performance compared with a GPU. CPUs are simply not meant for pixels.

So, why are GPUs so fast at processing fragments, pixels, and vertices compared to a CPU? The answer is that by the scalar nature of a CPU, it always process one instruction after another. On the other side, GPUs process hundreds of instructions simultaneously. A CPU has few (or only one) big multipurpose cores that can execute one shader's instance at once, but a GPU has dozens or hundreds of small and very specific cores that execute many shaders' instances in parallel.

Another great advantage of GPU over CPU is that all native types are vectorial. Imagine a typical CPU structure for a vector of floats:

```
struct Vector3
{
   float x, y, z;
};
```

Now suppose that you want to calculate the cross product of two vectors:

```
vec3 a;
vec3 b = {1, 2, 3};
vec3 c = {1, 1, 1};
// a = cross(b, c);
a.x = (b.y * c.z) - (b.z * c.y);
a.y = (b.z * c.x) - (b.x * c.z);
a.z = (b.x * c.y) - (b.y * c.x);
```

As you can see, this simple scalar operation in CPU took six multiplications, three subtractions, and three assignments; whereas in a GPU, vectorial types are native. A vec3 type is like a float or an int for a CPU. Also native types' operations are native too.

```
vec3 b = vec3(1, 2, 3);
vec3 c = vec3(1, 1, 1);
vec3 a = cross(b, c);
```

And that is all. The cross product operation is done in a single and atomic operation. This is a pretty simple example, but now think in the number of operations of these kinds that are done to process vertices and fragments per second and how a CPU would handle that. The number of multiplications and additions involved in a 4 x 4 matrix multiplication is quite large, while in GPU, it's only a matter of one single operation.

In a GPU, there are many other built-in operations (directly native or based on native operations) for native types: addition, subtraction, dot products, and inner/outer multiplications, geometric, trigonometric, or exponential functions. All these built-in operations are mapped directly (totally or partially) into the graphics hardware and therefore, all of them cost only a small fraction of the CPU equivalents.

All shader computations rely heavily on linear algebra calculations, mostly used to compute things such as light vectors, surface normals, displacement vectors, refractions and diffractions, cube maps, and so on. All these computations and many more are vector-based, so it is easy to see why a GPU has great advantages over a CPU to perform these tasks.

The following are the reasons why GPUs are faster than CPUs for vectorial calculations and graphics computations:

- Many shaders can be executed at the same time
- Inside a shader, many instructions can be executed in a block

The shader environment

Other applications that you might have coded in the past are built to run inside a CPU. This means that you have used a compiler that took your program (programmed in your favorite high-level programming language) and compiled it down into a representation that a CPU could understand. It does not matter if the programming language is compiled or interpreted, because in the end, all programs are translated to something the CPU can deal with.

Shaders are a little different because they are meant only for graphics, so they are closely related to the following two points:

- First, they need a graphics card, because inside the graphics card lies the processor that will run them. This special kind of processor is called the GPU (Graphics Processing Unit).
- A piece of software to reach the GPU: the GPU driver.

If you are going to program shaders, the first thing that you have to do is prepare your development environment, and that starts by downloading, and always keeping your graphics card driver updated.

Now suppose you are ready to start and have your first shader finished. You should compile and pass it to the GPU for execution. As GLSL relies on OpenGL, you must use OpenGL to compile and execute the shader. OpenGL has specific API calls for shader compilation: link, execution, and debug. Your OpenGL application now acts as a host application, from where you can manage your shaders and the resources that they might need, like for instance: textures, vertices, normals, framebuffers, or rendering states.

Summary

In this chapter, we learnt that there exists other worlds beyond the CPUs: GPUs and parallel computation. We also learnt how the internals of a graphics rendering pipeline are, which parts is it composed of, and a brief understanding of their functions.

In the next chapter, we will face the details of the language that controls the pipeline; a bit of grammar, and a bit of syntax.

2
GLSL Basics

OpenGL Shading Language is based on ANSI C. Many features of the **C programming language** have been incorporated to GLSL, while the ones that go against performance or language simplicity have been removed.

All GLSL shader types (vertex, fragment, geometry, and compute) use the same language, so you will benefit a lot from this chapter. All you will learn in this chapter will serve for every following chapter. In this chapter you will learn the basics of the language and the common elements between each shader type. Specifically, we will talk about the following topics:

- Language basics
- Shader input/ouput variables

Because GLSL is very close to the C language, I won't expose a complete and exhaustive list of each language element. I'll focus only on the differences between GLSL and C, and the biggest difference of them all, which will definitely lighten up a lot of readers, is that GLSL does not have pointers.

The Language

When you start coding a shader, you have to keep in mind one important thing: which GLSL version you are going to code for. This is usually a *minimum requirements* decision for your application. GLSL version is always bound to a specific OpenGL version, so in order to choose a GLSL version that supports the features we need, we are also tied to the minimum OpenGL version that supports that GLSL version.

At the moment of writing this book, I had to decide which version of GLSL to use. As we will talk about the compute shaders, we need to go to the minimum version that support them in a native way (not through extensions), and that's GLSL Version 4.30.6.

The official GLSL specification could be a good reference resource, once you have finished reading this book. You will be able to find the full list of functions in the tables located in the specification. The 4.30.6 GLSL specification can be downloaded directly from the OpenGL official site: `https://www.opengl.org/registry/doc/GLSLangSpec.4.30.8.pdf`.

Also, I'll focus only on the GLSL Core Profile, Forward Compatible. This is the cleanest way for someone who is new to GLSL; Core Profile, Forward Compatible ensures that deprecated elements won't be available for the programmer. There are OpenGL mechanisms such as display lists or the immediate drawing mode that are discouraged to use, but still remain in the language. Core Profile, Forward Compatible prevents their use by producing compilation or runtime errors if they are used.

Language basics

Before we begin, I expect you to have a basic understanding and proficiency of C. OpenGL is available in different programming languages such as Java, Python, or C#. However, I will be concentrating on the C/GLSL concepts.

Instructions

The instructions always end with a semicolon, and there could be more than one per line:

```
c = cross(a, b);
vec4 g; g = vec4(1, 0, 1, 1);
```

A block of instructions is created by putting them in brackets. All variables declared inside a block will be destroyed when the block finishes. If two variables have the same name—one declared outside the block (also called scope) and another declared inside the block—by default, the inner variable is the one which will be referenced:

```
float a = 1.0;
float b = 2.0;
{
  float a = 4.0;
  float c = a + 1.0; // c -> 4.0 + 1.0
}
b = b + c; // wrong statement. Variable c does not exist here
```

Tabulations or whitespaces don't change the semantics of the language. You can use them to format the code at your wish.

Basic types

GLSL is very rich regarding its basic types. In addition to standard C types, some others—mainly to represent vectors or expose the internal GPU architecture—have been added.

The following is the complete basic types list:

- `bool`: This can only have two possible values—`true` or `false`
- `int`: The two types of `int` are as follows:
    - `int` (normal integer value)
    - `uint` (unsigned integer value)
- `sampler` (types that represent textures):
    - `sampler1D`, `sampler2D`, `sampler3D`
- `float`
- Vectors:
    - `bvec2`, `bvec3`, `bvec4` (vectors of 2, 3, and 4 Boolean elements)
    - `ivec2`, `ivec3`, `ivec3` (vectors of 2, 3, and 4 integer elements)
    - `uvec2`, `uvec3`, `uvec4` (vectors of 2, 3, and 4 unsigned integers)
    - `vec2`, `vec3`, `vec4` (vectors of 2, 3, and 4 floats, single precision)
    - `dvec2`, `dvec3`, `dvec4` (vectors of 2, 3, and 4 floats, and double precision)
- Matrices: Matrices are always made of floating point numbers (the `d` prefix stands for double precision):
    - `mat2`, `mat3`, `mat4` (2 x 2, 3 x 3, and 4 x 4 matrices)
    - `dmat2`, `dmat3`, `dmat4` (2 x 2, 3 x 3, and 4 x 4 matrices)
    - `mat2x3`, `mat2x4`, `mat3x2`, `mat3x4`, `mat4x2`, `mat4x3` (first number refers to columns and second to rows)
    - `dmat2x3`, `dmat2x4`, `dmat3x2`, `dmat3x4`, `dmat4x2`, `dmat4x3` (first number refers to columns, second to rows)

On the contrary to C/C++, when writing `float` literals, if you don't put the suffix `f`, the compiler understands that the literal is `float`. To specifically write a double-precision literal, you must use the suffix `1f` or `1F`:

- `1.5`: float, single precision
- `1.3945958`: float, single precision
- `1.903945f`: float, single precision
- `1.3904859045F`: float, single precision
- `1.51F`: double precision
- `1.340950431f`: double precision

Variable initializers

To initialize or assign a value to a variable, you must use the constructor of the type to the variable. Let's see some examples:

```
float a = 1.0;
bool switch = false;  // Ok
ivec3 a = ivec3(1, 2, 3);  // Ok
uvec2 a = uvec2(-1, 2);  // Error, uivec2 is unsigned
vec3 a(1.0, 2.0);  // Error, you must assign the constructor
vec3 a = vec3(1.0, 2.0);  // Ok
```

A very useful trick about vector initialization is that there are a lot of constructors available. For example, you can construct `vec4` from `vec3` and `float`, or two `vec2`, or `float` and `vec3`. All possible combinations of elements that, in the end, fit in size with the target constructor are available:

```
vec4 a = vec4(1.0, vec3(0.0, 1.0, 0.0));
vec4 a = vec4(vec3(0.0, 1.0, 0.0), 0.9);
vec4 a = vec4(vec2(1.0, 1.0), vec2(0.5, 0.5));
```

A vector can be seen as structures or arrays. The structure's fields of a vector are predefined by the language, and the array sizes are the expected just looking at the type name (the size of `vec3` is 3).

For vectors, the following are the valid names for the structure's fields (the three groups are synonymous):

- {x, y, z, w} useful when accessing vectors that represent positions
- {r, g, b, a} useful when accessing vectors that represent colors
- {s, t, p, q} useful when accessing vectors that represent texture coordinates

Also, you can index the vectors using subscripts:

```
vec2 p;
p[0] = 1.0; // ok
p.x = 1.0; // Ok
p.y = 2.0; // Ok
p.z = 3.0; // Illegal, p is a vec2, only has 2 elements
```

GLSL allows you to **swizzle** the components of a vector (that is, construct a new vector by duplicating or reordering the elements of the former). To make this possible, GLSL allows things so useful like the next ones:

```
vec4 color1 = vec4(0.5, 0.2, 1.0, 1.0); // RGBA color;

// Let's convert color to abgr
vec4 color2 = color1.abgr; // equivalent to color1.wzyx

// Let's make a grey color based only on the red component
vec4 redGray = color1.rrrr;
float red = color1.r;

// Let's swizzle randomly but in valid way
vec4 color3 = color1.gbgb;
Vec4 color4 = vec4(color1.rr, color2.bb); // .rr .bb are vec2
Vec4 color5 = color1.tptp; // the same than .gbgb
vec4 color6 = color1.yzyz; // the same than .gbgb and .tptp
color6.xy = vec2(1.0, 0.0);
color6[3] = 2.0;

// Some invalid swizzles
vec2 p;
p = color1.rgb; // .rgb is vec3
p.xyz = color.rgb; // .xyz doesn't match p's size
p[2] = 3.0; // index out of bounds.
vec4 color7 = color1.xxqq; // Ilegal, components don't come from the
same set
```

Talking about matrices, they follow the same rules as compared to vectors, except the fact that a matrix is an array of column vectors and GLSL matrices are column matrices. This means that the first subscript is the column index and the second subscript is the row index:

```
mat4 m;
m[0] = vec4(1.0); // put the first column to 1.0 in each element
m[1][1] = 2.0; // put the second diagonal element to 2.0
m[2] = color3.xxyy; // Insert a swizzled vector into the third column
```

Vector and matrix operations

By default, the vector and matrix operations and some arithmetic operators have been overloaded in order to match linear algebraic conventions. Almost all operations are component-wise, but multiplications of matrix by matrix and matrix by vector follows the rules of the linear algebraic transforms:

```
mat3 R, T, M;
vec3 v, b;
float f;
// Initialize f, b, v, R and T with some values
// …

// Component wise example
b = v + f;
/* this stands for:
b.x = v.x + f;
b.y = v.y + f;
b.z = v.z + f;
The same is applied with the product operator, even between two vector
types */

// Linear algebra transform
// Vectors are considered column vectors
b = T * v;
/* Is equivalent to:
b.x = T[0].x * v.x + T[1].x * v.y + T[2].x * v.z;
b.y = T[0].y * v.x + T[1].y * v.y + T[2].y * v.z;
b.z = T[0].z * v.x + T[1].z * v.y + T[2].z * v.z; */

M = T * R;
/* Too long for putting that operation here, but it follows the rules
of column matrices*/
```

Summarizing, and talking about transform matrices, if you want to transform a vector with a transform matrix, just post-multiply it. If you want to concatenate transforms, just write them naturally from right to left:

```
b = T * v; // Translate v with the translation matrix T
b = R * T * v; // Translate and then rotate vector v
vertex = projection * modelview * vertex_position;

/* Transform a vertex position from model coordinates to clip
coordinate system. This is the way we always will go from model space
to clip space.*/
```

Castings and conversions

You can only cast types to other types when there won't be precision issues in the process, but other types of casts must be done explicitly. For example, you can cast implicitly from int to uint, from int to float, from float to double, and so on.

Otherwise, you must perform casts explicitly or you will end up with compilation errors. Explicit casting is done through a constructor. For example:

```
float threshold = 0.5;
int a = int(threshold); // decimal part is dropped, so a = 0;
double value = 0.3341f
float value2 = float(value);
bool c = false;
value2 = float(c); // value2 = 0.0;
c = true;
value2 = float(c); // value2 = 1.0;
```

In general, if you have problems with implicit castings, switch to the explicit way (or better, always do explicit conversions).

Code comments

Code comments are useful for making annotations in the code to clarify some operations for further readings. It isn't unusual to find coding a bit too tedious if you take a break from it for a while. Under such scenarios, it is always better to include comments for referencing later. There are two code comments styles: single-line comments or block of lines comments:

```
// This is a single-line comment. This line will be ignored by the
compiler

/* This is a block of lines comment. It's initialized
   with a slash and an asterisk and ends with an asterisk
   and slash. Inside this block you can put anything, but
   be careful because these kind of comments can't be nested */
```

Flow control

Just as with almost all other programming languages, you can control the flow of your code by checking Boolean conditions:

```
if(a > threshold)
   ligthColor = vec4(1.0, 1.0, 1.0, 1.0); //single new line, no
   matter the indentation
```

Alternatively, place the next code statement in the same line:

```
if(a > threshold) lightColor = vec4(1.0, 1.0, 1.0, 1.0);
```

You can also use the `else` statement to perform actions when the `if` condition is not true:

```
if(a > threshold)
   lightColor = vec4(1.0, 1.0, 1.0, 1.0);
else
   lightColor = vec4(1.0, 0.0, 0.0, 1.0); // when a <= threshold
```

The last variant is for when you want to test some conditions using the same range, for example, when using one or more `else` `if` statements:

```
if(a < threshold)
   lightColor = vec4(1.0, 0.0, 0.0, 1.0);
else if(a == threshold)
   lightColor = vec4(0.0, 1.0, 0.0, 1.0);
else if((a > threshold + 1) && (a <= threshold + 2))
   lightColor = vec4(0.0, 0.0, 1.0, 1.0);
else
   lightColor = vec4(1.0, 1.0, 1.0, 1.0);
```

The C-like languages are not indentation based, such as Python for example. If you want to specify more than one instruction, you have to explicitly use blocks:

```
if(a > threshold)
{
   lightColor = vec4(1.0, 1.0, 1.0, 1.0);
   baseColor = vec4(1.0, 0.0, 0.0, 1.0);
}
```

Of course, you can nest conditionals as in any other programming language. In GLSL, it is perfectly fine and legal (but bad for performance, as conditionals always are):

```
if(a > threshold1)
{
   if(b > threshold2)
   {
      LightColor = vec4(1.0, 0.0, 0.0, 1.0);
   }
   lightColor = vec4(0.0, 1.0, 0.0, 1.0);
}
else
   lightColor = vec4(0.0, 0.0, 0.0, 1.0);
```

When you need to check different possibilities of a single variable's value, you could use the switch-case statement:

```
switch(myVariable)
{
  case 1: // when myVariable's value is 1
    lightColor = vec4(1.0, 0.0, 0.0, 1.0);
    break;
  case 2: // when myVariable's value is 2
    lightColor = vec4(0.0, 1.0, 0.0, 1.0);
    break;
  case 3: // when myVariable's value is 3
    lightColor = vec4(0.0, 0.0, 1.0, 1.0);
    break;
  default: // in any other case.
    lightColor = vec4(1.0, 1.0, 1.0, 1.0);
}
```

There are a few things to explain here. First, you must have noticed the break statement. You have to put it there to separate the cases. If you don't, and suppose case 2 has no break statement, code execution will continue into case 3.

 Don't forget to put breaks wherever necessary.

I also have put the default clause there. This clause is where the code will be when all the other cases fail. In this example, if the value of myVariable is 4, 5, or 42342344, the code will enter in the default clause. This clause is optional, so you don't have to put it there if you don't need it.

A switch-case statement is equivalent to a chain of if-else if statements; but if you can, use the switch statement instead of if-else.

switch **statement**	if-else **statement**
``switch(a)
{
case 1:
offset = offset + 1.3;
offset2 = offset;
break;
case 2:
offset = offset + 3.4;
break;
default:
offset = 0;
}```	```if(a == 1)
{
offset = offset + 1.3;
offset2 = offset;
}
else if(a == 2)
offset = offset + 3.4;
else
offset = 0;```

Loops

In GLSL, we have the three most commonly used loops in programming, `for`, `while`, and `do while`.

The `for` loop is the most common one. It has three blocks, and all of them are optional—initialization, finalization condition check, and the increment counter block—and all of them are separated with semicolons:

```
for(initialization; check-condition; increment)
```

The instructions of the loop could be a single instruction or a block of instructions (this will apply to the other loops):

```
for(float i = 0.0; i < 10.0; i = i + 1.0)
{
   myVariable = myVariable + i * 1.3;
}
```

This loop will repeat ten times. Firstly, the variable `i` is created and initialized. Then, once the condition is checked, the `for` body is executed and `i` is incremented. This is repeated until the value of `i` is 9, because `i` will be increased in the next check.

Finally, the condition will fail when `i` is larger than or equal to `10.0`, terminating the execution of the loop.

The `while` loop is somehow simpler than the `for` loop. It checks a condition, and if that condition is true, it executes the loop's body; if not, the loop ends:

```
float i = 0.0;
while(i < 10.0)
{
   myVariable = myVariable + i * 1.3;
   i = i + 1.0;
}
```

 The condition check is executed before the loop's body. This is done to avoid the body's execution when the condition is initially false.

The last loop provided by GLSL is do-while. It's very similar to the while loop, but with a big difference: the condition is executed after the loop's body:

```
float i = 0.0;
do
{
  myVariable = myVarialble + i * 1.3;
  j = j + 1.0;
}while(i < 10.0f)
```

 Because the condition is tested after the loop's body is executed, it will be executed always at least once.

Remember, this loop isn't equivalent at all to the while loop. Use it only when you explicitly need the loop's body to be executed at least once.

Structures

Ok, at this point we have some useful variable types—int, float, and so on—but those are plain numerical representations. What if we have to represent something from the real world with a variable? We need to create a new variable type that contains in some manner the properties of the object we want to represent. For that purpose we have structures.

A structure is simply a collection of other types under a custom name. For example, we can say that a surface material (for our purposes) is composed of a base texture color, roughness coefficient, and a tint color, so let's define that new type:

```
struct MySurface
{
  vec3 baseTextureColor; // RGB color
  float roughness;
  vec3 tint;   // RGB Color
};
```

 Notice the trailing semicolon after the closing bracket; it's mandatory by the language's syntax.

Inside a structure declaration, you can put any existing type, or even other custom structures. Now, in order to use this new type, we only have to declare a variable of this new type:

```
MySurface tableSurface;
```

And, to access individual elements, just put the variable name, a dot, and the field name you want access to:

```
tableSurface.roughness = 2.0;
```

You can also initialize the whole structure in one step:

```
MySurface surface = MySurface(vec3(1.0, 1.0, 1.0), 0.5, vec3(1.0,
    0.0, 0.0));
```

Just remember, place the initialization field's values in the same order of the structure declaration.

Arrays

Now, what if you need to treat many variables of the same type in a generic way? You can arrange them in an array and use the same name for all of them, but accessing individual elements with an index.

To do this, just declare the variable and put the number (it has to be a number that can be resolved at compile time) of instances inside square brackets:

```
float coefficient[4];
MySurface surfaces[3];
for(float i = 0; i < 4; i = i + 1.0)
{
/* Be careful with the index. If it becomes larger than the declared
number of instances, it will make the shader crash at runtime */
    coefficient[i] = i * 2.0;
}

for(float i = 0; i < 3; i = i + 1.0)
{
    surfaces[i].roughness = i * + 1.2;
}
```

Arrays and vectors also have the useful property `.length()`, which returns the number of elements of the array:

```
for(int i = 0; i < coefficient.length(); ++i)
{
  // Do whatever
}
```

Also, you can statically initialize an array directly in the declaration:

```
float myArray[] = {1.0, 2.0, 3.0, 4.0};
vec2 myArray2[] = {vec2(0.0, 0.0), vec2(1.0,0.0), vec2(1.0, 1.0)};
```

Functions

Now you have the basic language structures to build a simple program. In fact, you have everything you would need, but when a program reaches a certain size, it's always useful to break it into functional parts. Sometimes, you will break the program to reuse code and avoid repeating it everywhere if it's a common operation or for code clarity and readability.

Let's put a simple example, just to show the features that I want to show:

```
// Structure declaration, to use as sample
struct Light
{
  vec3 position;
  vec3 diffuseColor;
  vec3 attenuation;
};

// Shader entry point, just like in C, but no input params
void main()
{
  vec3 myPosition = vec3(1.0, 0.0, 0.0);

  // Let's create and initialize some ligths
  Light light1 = Light(vec3(10.0, 0.0, 0.0), vec3(1.0, 0.0, 0.0),
    vec3(1.0, 2.0, 3.0));
  Light light2 = Light(vec3(0.0, 10.0, 0.0), vec3(1.0, 0.0, 0.0) ,
    vec3(1.0, 2.0, 3.0));
  Light light3 = Light(vec3(0.0, 0.0, 10.0), vec3(1.0, 0.0, 0.0) ,
    vec3(1.0, 2.0, 3.0));
```

```
   // Calculate simplified light contribution and add to final color
   vec3 finalColor = vec3(0.0, 0.0, 0.0);
   //distance is a GLSL built-in function
   float distance1 = distance(myPosition, light1.position);
   float attenuation1 = 1.0 / (light1.attenuation[0] + light1.
     attenuation[1] * distance1 + light1.attenuation[2] *
     distance1 * distance1);
   finalColor += light1.diffuseColor * light1.attenuation;

   // Let's calculate the same, for light2
   float distance2 = distance(myPosition, light2.position);
   float attenuation2 = 1.0 / (light2.attenuation[0] + light2.
     attenuation[1] * distance2 + light2.attenuation[2] *
     distance2 * distance2);
   finalColor += light2.diffuseColor * light2.attenuation;

   // Light 3
   float distance3 = distance(myPosition, light3.position);
   float attenuation3 = 1.0 / (light3.attenuation[0] + light3.
     attenuation[1] * distance3 + light3.attenuation[2] * distance3 *
     distance3);
   finalColor += light3.diffuseColor * light3.attenuation;

   // Now finalColor stores our desired color
}
```

As you can see, I repeated the same operations three times, once per light; this is a bad idea. It is very error-prone, and hardly debuggeable, and if you continue this way, your shaders will be bloated with repetitive code. The point here is to use a function to calculate the light contribution in a desired point and add that value to the final color, which I'll show you in the next example:

```
struct Light
{
  vec3 position;
  vec3 diffuseColor;
vec3 attenuation;
};

vec3 CalculateContribution(const in Light light, const in vec3
position)
{
float distance = distance(position, light.position);
  float attenuation = 1.0 / (light.attenuation[0] + light.
    attenuation[1] * distance + light.attenuation[2] * distance *
    distance);
```

```
      return light.diffuseColor * light.attenuation;
}
// Shader entry point, just like in C, but no input params
void main()
{
  vec3 myPosition = vec3(1.0, 0.0, 0.0);
  Light light1 = Light(vec3(10.0, 0.0, 0.0), vec3(1.0, 0.0, 0.0) ,
    vec3(1.0, 2.0, 3.0));

  Light light2 = Light(vec3(0.0, 10.0, 0.0), vec3(1.0, 0.0, 0.0) ,
    vec3(1.0, 2.0, 3.0));
  Light light3 = Light(vec3(0.0, 0.0, 10.0), vec3(1.0, 0.0, 0.0) ,
    vec3(1.0, 2.0, 3.0));

  // Calculate light1
  vec3 finalColor = CalculateContribution(light1, myPosition);
  // Calculate light2
  finalColor += CalculateContribution(light2, myPosition);
  // Calculate light3
  finalColor += CalculateContribution(light3, myPosition);
}
```

As you can see, the code is now much more readable, and if you have an error in the light's formula, you only have to fix it in one place.

Now, let's go into more detail with function usage and creation. First of all, a function must be defined or declared before you can use it. If not, you will get a compile-time error. You can achieve this by simply putting the function before the point where you will use it, or putting its definition (the prototype) before the use point and declare it later.

The following is the function prototype:

```
vec3 CalculateContribution(const in Light light, const in vec3
  position);
```

As usual in C, the first keyword is the return type, and in this case, this function returns vec3. If you aren't going to return any value, you must use void instead.

This function receives a Light type variable and a vec3 variable as input. The keyword const means that the variable will not be modified inside the function. The keyword in means that after the function call, the variable will remain unchanged, no matter what you did inside the function. The keyword out means that the variable will only be copied out but not copied in, and the keyword inout means that the variable will be copied in and copied out by the function.

[The out variables are not initialized when passed in a function.]

Of course, the const qualifier doesn't have meaning with the out or inout qualifiers, so you can't use that combination.

By default, if no in/out/inout qualifiers are specified, in is the one which is implicitly used.

[GLSL does not provide pointers. You must use the in/out/inout qualifiers to pass variables by value or by reference to functions.]

Preprocessor

Like in C, GLSL has a **preprocessor**. The preprocessor is a precompilation step over the shader's source code (prior to the compilation step that transforms the GLSL program into machine code) that executes simple string substitution, among other things such as reading compilation directives. Basically, it scans the code looking for some tags that will be evaluated and replaced by real values.

All preprocessor tags start with the character # (hashtag), and the most important ones are:

- #error
- #version
- #pragma
- #define
- #if, #ifdef, #ifndef, #else, #elif, #endif

The #error directive will display the message that is next to the keyword in the shader's compilation log, and will also produce a compilation error. If the preprocessor reaches an #error directive, the shader will be considered ill-formed and not executable:

```
#ifndef DEG2RAD
   #error missing conversion macro
#endif
```

The #version directive is meant to force the compiler to stick to a certain GLSL version. It has to be placed in the first line of the shader.

This is very useful because it ensures better compatibility. If you want to use only the feature set of a certain GLSL version (for example, to avoid deprecated things in your shader code), this is critical because the compiler will throw you an error when it detects that you are using newer or older GLSL features than the version you actually have specified.

In all of our shaders, our first line will be `#version 430`.

The `#pragma` directive is meant to provide some information to the GLSL compiler. With this directive, you can put the shader in debug/release mode (`#pragma debug(on)`, `#pragma debug(off)`) or turn on or off optimizations (`#pragma optimize(on)`, `#pragma optimize(off)`). By default, the pragma optimization is enabled while debug is turned off.

I suggest using `debug (on)` pragma always because this way we will have more information from the compiler when errors occur. Also, `optimize (off)` pragma is very useful when debugging, because the compiler, from time to time, makes mistakes optimizing the code, and you could spend hours or days debugging a problem that is not your fault. Enable optimization for production environments and check that it works exactly like the non-optimized version (but faster!).

The `#define` directive defines a preprocessor symbol, optionally assigning it a value. Fake parameters could be used to create pseudo functions (macros). The `#undef` directive removes that symbol from the list of defined preprocessor symbols.

The `#if` and `#endif` directives enables or disables code. If the condition of the `#if` directive is true, the code between `#if` and `#endif` is compiled. If it's false, the code between `#if` and `#endif` is removed from the source code, and therefore not compiled.

As with normal programming language ifs, we have else (`#else`), else if (`#elif`), and the closing directive (`#endif`), needed because we don't use brackets here.

The `#ifdef` directive is a little special, because it doesn't check a Boolean expression. It checks if the preprocessor symbol that is next to `#ifdef` has been declared or not (`#ifndef` checks if the symbol has *not* been declared).

Some examples will clarify the usage. Let's make a generic shader function:

```
// Let's ensure we run the GLSL version 4.30
#version 430
#pragma debug(on)
#pragma optimize(off)
```

```
// Let's define PI, but first, if it were defined, we will undefined
it, to use a new value
#ifdef PI
#undef PI
#endif
#define PI 3.141592

/* define a macro to convert degrees to radians. Notice that we
   are using the previously defined PI macro. Comment out or uncomment
the next line to see the effect of #ifdef few lines below */
#define DEG2RAD(x) ((x) * PI / 180.0)

// a sample macro
#define NUMBER_OF_TEXTURES 2

void main()
{
  float degrees = 45.0;
  /* if the DEG2RAD macro exists, we will use it, if not, we
   will calculate the radians by our means */
  #ifdef DEG2RAD
  float cosine2 = cos(DEG2RAD(degrees));
  #else
    float cosine = cos(degrees * PI / 180.0);
  #endif

  // Just to show how #if works... nothing to explain.
  vec4 color;
  #if NUMBER_OF TEXTURES == 2
    color = ReadTextureColor(2);
    color += ReadTextureColor(1);
  #elif NUMBER_OF_TEXTURES == 1
    color = ReadTextureColor(1);
  #elif NUMBER_OF_TEXTURES == 0
    color = vec4(0.0, 0.0, 0.0, 1.0);
  #else
  // We'd detected an error! let's stop the compilation here.
  #error Unsupported number of textures
  #endif
}
```

Once the preprocessor has done its work, the code that will be compiled in the next stage will be the following:

```
#version 430
#pragma debug(on)
#pragma optimize(off)

void main()
{
    float degrees = 45.0;
    float cosine2 = cos(((degrees) * 3.141592 / 180.0));

    vec4 color;
    color = ReadTextureColor(2);
    color += ReadTextureColor(1);
}
```

Shader input and output variables

Until now, we've been speaking about the language itself; how it's similar to the C programming language, but focusing specially on the differences. That was only the language part. Now it's time to see some of the functional parts of GLSL and cover an important topic: the inputs and outputs of the shaders.

Uniform variables

Suppose, you want to create a shader that makes use of a simple light. Well, shaders don't know about lights or any other high-level concept. Shaders only know about math and programming. So, if the language doesn't have support for lights, how would I use the light's position or color in a shader?

You need to pass those variables from your application to your shader and perform the lighting calculations inside the shader.

A parameter that is passed from the application to the shaders is called a **uniform** variable. Those variables are always read-only (constant), global to the shaders that form the current executable program.

The procedure is the following: first, set up the uniform's value, draw some triangles, change the variable (if desired), draw other triangles, and repeat this process until you're finished with your rendering.

As a quick note, this is how you'd set the uniform variable's values in the host program (the following lines of code are C and OpenGL, not GLSL).

Once your shader has been compiled, linked, and activated, you need to find the variable's index (location):

```
// C code to initialize a Uniform variable.
// programID = OpenGL program id, "lightPosition" = name of the
variable inside the shader. It's case sensitive, so be careful
int location = glGetUniformLocation(programID, "lightPosition");

// Let's create a dummy position, an array of 3
float myLight1Position[] = {0, 10.0f, 0};

// Set the values into the uniform's slot
glUniform3fv(location, myLight1Position);
```

With this, we have filled the uniform variable with the valid values. Now let's go to the shader's part:

 If you do not give a value to a variable before the shader is used, the variable's value is undefined.

```
#version 430
#pragma debug(on)
#pragma optimize(off)

uniform vec3 lightPosition;
void main()
{
    // Do your calculations here with lightPosition
}
```

You can pass whatever you want as a uniform variable: single integers, matrices, structures, or even arrays of structures.

Other input variables

There are other types of input variables, and all of them are meant to connect between different pipeline stages. Each has a purpose, and their usage differs depending on where they are going to be used. Let's see how to define them using an example, but this would be covered in depth in corresponding chapters.

The input variables are global variables, like the uniforms are, and must be declared globally in the shader with the keyword `in`.

There are several qualifiers, mostly related with precision, interpolation modes, or for other shader-type-specific matters. But to keep things simple, we won't care about those qualifiers right now. I'll use a fragment shader as an example:

```
#version 430
// Don't care about smooth keyword right now.
in smooth vec3 vertexColor;

// Color that will be written into the framebuffer
out vec4 frameBufferColor;
void main()
{
   frameBufferColor = vec4(vertexColor, 1.0);
}
```

In the last shader (which is a basic fragment shader actually), `vertexColor` is an input variable that holds a vertex interpolated color that was previously an output from a vertex shader.

Shader output variables

Every shader is meant to perform work, and always the result of that work must be in the form of an output. In the case of a fragment shader, the output is at least the color of a fragment. In the case of a vertex shader, the output is at least the vertex position in clip coordinates, and usually some other vertex attributes that will be interpolated and passed to the fragment shader.

Besides, all qualifiers that GLSL provides for those kinds of variables, the important keyword here is `out`. As with the input variables, the output variables must be declared globally. In the case of fragment shaders, the semantics of `out` means that the variable will contain (in most cases) the color that will be drawn in the framebuffer.

 A fragment shader could output other things besides the color, such as the fragment's depth or separated colors for multiple framebuffers simultaneously, but we will talk mostly about single colors as fragment shader output.

Summary

We have learned about all the tools that we need to start reading about specific shaders. Although, this chapter contains plenty of new definitions and concepts, it contains the minimum (but solid) base to start developing shaders.

We learned about language grammar, key C-GLSL differences, basic language structures, shaders' native vectorial types and operations, and shaders' inputs and outputs. Now, in the next chapter, we will face our first true challenge: vertex shaders.

3
Vertex Shaders

Vertex shaders are responsible for transforming the incoming geometry into something suitable to be rasterized, according to the rendering pipeline laws. In order to make this work, a vertex shader's inputs and outputs must be very well defined.

In this chapter we will see how the inputs must be prepared and how we can compute the outputs. Also, we will talk extensively about the operations we are allowed to perform.

A vertex shader executes once and only once for each vertex sent to the GPU. Inside a vertex shader, you have access to all information about that vertex, but you can't access the other sibling vertices of the primitive that is being processed.

It doesn't matter for the vertex shader which type of primitive and how you had arranged it before sending it to the GPU (indexed, non-indexed, interleaved, non-interleaved, VBO, VAO, and so on).

So, in the end, a vertex shader is a "give me one vertex that I'll transform for you" machine, and nothing else. Things have been kept simple as you can see.

We will finish this chapter with an example where we'll talk about possible problems, solutions, and debugging techniques when you don't get the expected results.

Vertex shader inputs

A vertex shader can have only two different kinds of inputs: vertex attributes and uniform variables.

Vertex attributes

A **vertex attribute** is simply the information you pass to the shader, in a per-vertex basis, along the plain vertex position in the world. Examples of vertex attributes could be:

- **Texture coordinates**
- **Normals**
- **Tangents**
- **Per-vertex colors**

Because of the evolving nature of OpenGL, version after version, details tend to be generalized. OpenGL specification writers try to define the data as uniform as possible. In the early programmable shader's days, there were specific attributes with specific names for texture coordinates, normals, vertex colors, and so on. Now, all attributes are generic and have no special names. They are simply vertex attribute buffers.

In order to show how attributes are bound to the vertex shader, we need to see how to set them up in the OpenGL host application.

First, we have to create and fill a vertex array configured with vertices and texture coordinates (for example). There are many ways to accomplish this. I'll present an interleaved **vertex array object** (**VAO**) that will hold one complete vertex in the buffer (position and texture coordinates) at once, so the buffer will look like XYZWSTXYZWST, with XYZW as the vertex position coordinates and ST as the texture coordinates:

```
// Create vertex array object (VAO)
glGenVertexArrays(1, &vaoID);
glBindVertexArray(vaoID);

// Create vertex buffer object (VBO)
glGenBuffers(1, &vboID);
glBindBuffer(GL_ARRAY_BUFFER, vboID);

// Fill buffer with data
glBufferData(GL_ARRAY_BUFFER, bufferElementsCount * sizeof(GLfloat),
bufferData, GL_STATIC_DRAW);

// Tell OpenGL how to locate the first attribute (positions) inside
the buffer
glEnableVertexAttribArray(0);
```

```
glVertexAttribPointer(0, 4, GL_FLOAT, GL_FALSE, (4 + 2)*
sizeof(GLfloat), NULL);

// Tell OpenGL how to locate the second attribute (texture
coordinates) inside the buffer
glEnableVertexAttribArray(1);
glVertexAttribPointer(1, 2, GL_FLOAT, GL_FALSE, (4 + 2) *
sizeof(float),(void*)(4 * sizeof(float)));

// Deactivate VAO
glBindBuffer(GL_ARRAY_BUFFER, 0);
glBindVertexArray(0);
```

In this code snippet, I have set up a VAO with two vertex attributes. In the attribute with index 0, I have placed the vertex positions, and in the array with index 1, the texture coordinates.

So, now that we have our data ready, let's get back to the shader. We need to know how to access our buffer from the vertex shader. Although there are some options for this, I always use the most explicit (and simplest) one. Recollecting the fact that I put positions in slot 0 and the texture coordinates in slot 1, I'll use the slot numbers to access data from the shader with that information. An empty vertex shader would look like the following:

```
#version 430
#pragma debug(on)
#pragma optimize(off)

// 0 -> the slot I set with the glEnableVertexAttribArray(0) call for
the vertices' positions
layout (location = 0) in vec4 position;

// 1 -> the slot I set with the glEnableVertexAttribArray(1) call for
the vertices' positions
layout (location = 1) in vec2 texCoords;

void main()
{
  // Do something here
}
```

As you can see, we've used the keyword `in`. Also, we're explicitly telling the shader in which slot we have placed the attributes. This way of specifying attributes could be good for your rendering system if you always use the same attributes layout, but if not, you have the option to let OpenGL automatically assign the slot and later query it.

Uniform variables

You can pass your application's single variables unrelated with the pipeline or with any other constraint. These variables' values are constant until you change their values from your OpenGL host application.

Using these variables, you can pass the transform matrices to the shader, lighting parameters, or whatever you can think of. Let's create our first working vertex shader with them.

First, let's upload the variables' values to the GPU in the OpenGL host application:

```
// Enable our shader program. Before doing any operation like setting
uniforms or retrieving vertex attribute slot numbers, the shader must
be activated/bound using this function
glUseProgram(programID);

// Value to be uploaded to the GPU
GLfloat mdlv[16] = …; // Fill with proper values
GLfloat proj[16] = …; // Fill with proper values

// retrieve variable's slots from the shader using the variable's
names in the shader
Glint location = glGetUniformLocation(programID, "Modelview");
// Upload the values to the shader
glUniformMatrix2fv(location, 1, GL_FALSE, mdlv);

location = glGetUniformLocation(programID, "Projection");
glUniformMatrix4fv(location, 1, GL_FALSE, proj);
```

And that's all. The values are ready to be used in the shader. Let's complete the GLSL example:

```
#version 430
#pragma debug(on)
#pragma optimize(off)

layout (location = 0) in vec4 Position;
```

```
// uniform matrices declaration. This must be done globally
uniform mat4 Modelview;
uniform mat4 Projection;

void main()
{
  // Let's compute the vertex position in clip coordinate system
  gl_Position = Projection * Modelview * Position;
}
```

Besides uploading a plain array of floats as uniform values, we have declared variables of the mat4 type. GLSL will take care of formatting those arrays into the target type automatically. Of course, the data must fit naturally. You can't simply map bool to mat4, or even float[9] to mat4. You must be careful with this.

gl_Position is a special (built-in) value that must hold the transformed vertex position. This is the only requirement for a vertex shader and is its main purpose. Not putting a value there will render your shader unusable and ill-formed and you will get a compiler error.

Vertex shader outputs

Vertex shaders can output generic values to the next stage. Those values are going to be passed to the geometry shading stage first, then rasterized, and finally passed to the fragment shading stage in one of the allowed interpolation fashions. You can choose the kind of interpolation, but we will use in this book a linear perspective-corrected interpolation.

To specify an output variable, you must use the interpolation type along with the out keyword:

```
#version 430
#pragma debug(on)
#pragma optimize(off)
layout (location = 0) in vec4 Position;
layout (location = 1) in vec2 TexCoord;

uniform mat4 Modelview;
uniform mat4 Projection;

// smooth = linearly perspective-correct interpolation
smooth out vec2 texCoordsInterpolated;
```

```
void main()
{
    gl_Position = Projection * Modelview * Position;

    // Write the vertex attribute into an output variable that will be
    interpolated in a later pipeline's stages
    texCoordsInterpolated = TexCoord;
}
```

Drawing a simple geometry sample

In order to have a runnable shader program, we need a vertex shader and a fragment shader. Until now, we have not spoken about fragment shaders, but we still need one to run the samples, so I'll present here a simple fragment shader to use in conjunction with the next vertex shaders. This will be our sample fragment shader, kept as simple as possible for learning purposes:

```
// Fragment shader
#version 430
#pragma debug(on)
#pragma optimize(off)

uniform vec4 SolidColor;

// Writing to this variable will set the current fragment's color
out vec4 frameBufferColor;

void main()
{
    frameBufferColor = SolidColor;
}
```

This fragment shader paints the whole triangle surface with a solid color, provided by means of a uniform variable (fragment shaders also have uniform variables).

Coming back to the vertex shaders, let's start with a simple one. The simplest thing we could want to do is show our geometry as it is, on the screen, rendered with a single solid color. So, we only have to transform our vertices using the corresponding matrices:

```
// Vertex shader
#version 430
#pragma debug(on)
#pragma optimize(off)

layout (location = 0) in vec4 position;

uniform mat4 Modelview;
uniform mat4 Projection;

void main()
{
   gl_Position = Projection * Modelview * position;
}
```

We can also compute projection modelview in the CPU and pass the result to the shader. We can stop it from being executed many times in the shader, because that multiplication always throws the same result (as long as both matrices don't change) for all primitives in our current OpenGL drawing call. So, our shader would look like the following:

```
// Vertex shader
#version 430
#pragma debug(on)
#pragma optimize(off)

layout (location = 0) in vec4 Position;

uniform mat4 ProjectionModelView;
void main()
{
   gl_Position = ProjectionModelView * Position;
}
```

If we compute the needed values' vertex positions for a teapot (or any other triangle mesh) and use this current sample's shader, passing a half red color in the uniform variable, we will get a render like the one in the following figure:

Distorting a geometry sample

OK, now that we have our geometry correctly rendered, let's perform some distortions on it. First, we will scale the teapot in the horizontal direction. We will need a scale matrix and to apply it to the geometry as the first transform to be applied:

```
// Vertex shader
#version 430
#pragma debug(on)
#pragma optimize(off)

layout (location = 0) in vec4 Position;

uniform mat4 ProjectionModelView;
void main()
{
  // Remember that the first vec4 is the first column, not the first
  row, although in the code apparently it looks like a row because of
  the way it's written
  mat4 scale = mat4(vec4(1, 0, 0, 0),// scale in the X direction
  vec4(0, 1, 0, 0),// scale in the y direction
  vec4(0, 0, 1, 0),// scale in the z direction
  vec4(0, 0, 0, 1));
  gl_Position = ProjectionModelView * scale * Position;
}
```

This shader has no deformation in the scale matrix. All scale factors are `1.0`, which means that all will remain in its original state. But look at the next figures when we change the scale factors:

To deform the **A** teapot, we have used the following scale matrix:

```
mat4 scale = mat4(vec4(1, 0, 0, 0),
  vec4(0, 1.5, 0, 0), // 150% scale in Y direction
  vec4(0, 0, 1, 0),
  vec4(0, 0, 0, 1));
For the (B) teapot, our matrix was:
mat4 scale = mat4(vec4(1.5, 0, 0, 0), // 150% scale in X direction
  vec4(0, 1, 0, 0),
  vec4(0, 0, 1, 0),
  vec4(0, 0, 0, 1));
And finally, the (C) teapot's scale matrix was:
mat4 scale = mat4(vec4(1, 0, 0, 0),
  vec4(0, 1, 0, 0),
  vec4(0, 0, 3, 0), // 300% scale in Z direction
  vec4(0, 0, 0, 1));
```

As you can see, just by applying the proper transform matrix, we get the desired deformation. Of course, there are other types of transform matrices: translations, rotations, and scales (and combinations of those) are the most widely used ones.

Using interpolators

Other output vertex values apart from `gl_Position` are often called **interpolators**. This is because the values stored there will be interpolated across the primitive's surface in the later stages. To explain this briefly, suppose that you are rendering a line. Then you want a different vertex color in each vertex, so you set up a vertex attribute array that stores those colors. Now suppose the color in the first vertex is pure white, and the color in the second vertex is pure black. If you put those vertex colors into an interpolator and pick that interpolated value in a fragment shader, each fragment to be painted will present an interpolated color between pure black and pure white. To summarize, the line you are drawing will form a gradient of grays, from pure white to pure black.

Using a 2D shape such as a quad and placing in each corner the values `(0,0)`, `(1,0)`, `(0,1)`, and `(1,1)`, we obtain the next diagram:

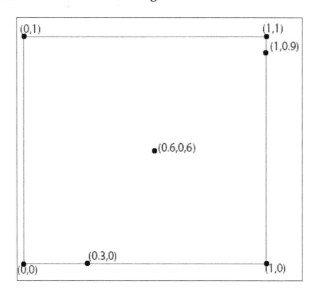

As you can see, the points that are generated in-between have been linearly interpolated; the closer to one corner, the closer the values.

The best way to visualize this is with colors. Let's render a triangle with a different color in each vertex: green in the left-bottom corner, right in the top corner, and blue in the bottom-right corner. The code for the same is as follows:

```
// Vertex shader
#version 430
#pragma debug(on)
#pragma optimize(off)
```

```
layout (location = 0) in vec4 Position;

// Vertexcolor buffer mapping
layout (location = 1) in vec4 VertexColor;

// Interpolator for our vertex color
smooth out vec4 interpolatedColor;

uniform mat4 ProjectionModelView;

void main()
{
  interpolatedColor = VertexColor;
  gl_Position = ProjectionModelView * scale * Position;
}

// Fragment shader
#version 430
#pragma debug(on)
#pragma optimize(off)

// Here we are receiving the interpolated vertex color
smooth in vec4 interpolatedColor;
out vec4 frameBufferColor;

void main()
{
  frameBufferColor = interpolatedColor;
}
```

This shader will produce the following rendering:

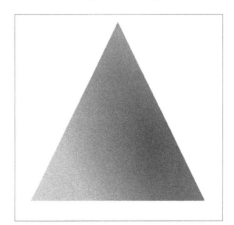

Simple lighting

Lighting is a quite extensive topic. You could write an entire book about this and you will only scratch the surface. There are so many techniques, from **flat shading** to **normal mapping**, passing through **ambient occlusion** or other **global illumination** techniques. We will talk in this section about how to prepare our vertex shaders to achieve, in the next chapter, convincing lighting effects using fragment shaders.

Basic lighting theory

First of all, I have to explain what comprises the **Phong** lighting model, because that's the one we base all our examples on, and nothing is better than a diagram for this purpose.

The Phong lighting model is a simple equation. It divides the light into three components:

- **Ambient**: This provides constant lighting contribution.
- **Diffuse**: This provides lighting contribution that depends on the light's position and the surface's point that is being lit (usually represented by a normal vector).
- **Specular**: This provides lighting contribution that depends on the light's position, the surface's point (normal), and the camera/viewer's position. This lighting component is a small and bright dot that appears on very reflective surfaces, such as metal or plastic.

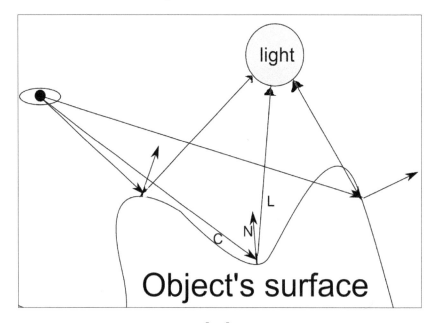

In our scenes, we would typically have a point of light, a camera (the eye), and an object to be lit. To illuminate each point of the object's surface, we need to know at least one important thing: the **normal vector** in that exact point (a normal vector is a normalized vector that is perpendicular to a surface's points). Let's call that vector N. We also need the vector that comes from the light and reaches the surface's point, as well as the vector that comes from the camera's position (the eye in the diagram).

According with this illumination model, the areas where the normal vectors are parallel to the light vectors will receive maximum lighting influence, and the areas where the angle between the normal vector and light vector are larger than 90 degrees won't be affected by light.

The camera's position affects only the specular component of the light. When we complete the lighting equation, this will be clear.

As you will see, the math will not be very involved, just a bit of linear algebra. Our main concern, and the decision that will define our illumination shader, will be how to compute the normal at each surface's point.

Depending on how we compute the triangles' normals, we will have different renderings:

- **Flat Shading**: This means we have the same normal for the whole triangle surface, and the same normal equates to the same lighting over the whole surface, so the triangle will be lit uniformly.
- **Gouraud Shading**: This uses only vertex normal computing's lighting contribution in the vertex shader and interpolates that contribution to the fragment shader.
- **Phong Shading**: This uses only vertex normals, which are interpolated across the triangle's surface to the fragment shader. Then, lighting is computed in the fragment shader using interpolated normals.

- **Normal mapping**: Normals come from a texture map; so, by fetching a normal from a texture, we get a very accurate normal for every fragment and not just an approximation by interpolation.

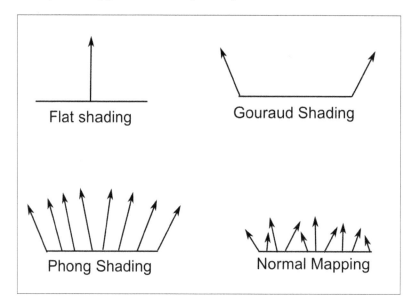

Lighting example code

Now to finish with lighting theory, let's introduce the lighting equation. In computer graphics, light is often divided into three (or more) independent elements that contribute to the final result. Those elements are, as said before, the ambient contribution, the diffuse contribution, and the specular contribution. I won't enter too deeply into these math equations, mainly because you can find the equations everywhere and because the point of this book is about shaders, not algorithms.

All three of these components are calculated and summed together to get the final lighting contribution at each point. Now, let's write down a vertex shader to produce a Gouraud lighting effect:

```
// Vertex shader
#version 430
#pragma debug(on)
#pragma optimize(off)

layout (location = 0) in vec4 Position;

// Vertex normals buffer mapping
layout (location = 1) in vec3 VertexNormal;
```

```
// Interpolator for our light
smooth out vec3 lightContribution;

/* Matrix to transform normals. This is the transpose of the
    inverse of the upper leftmost 3x3 of the modelview matrix */
uniform mat3 NormalMatrix;

uniform mat4 ModelView;
uniform mat4 Projection;

// We need to know where the light emitter is located
uniform vec3 LightPosition;

// The color of our light
uniform vec3 LightColor;

// Note: All vectors must always be normalized
void main()
{
  gl_Position = ProjectionModelView * Position;

  vec3 normal = normalize(NormalMatrix * VertexNormal);

  // Compute vertex position in camera coordinates
  vec4 worldVertexPos = ModelView * Position;

  // Compute the vector that comes from the light
  vec3 lightVec = normalize(LightPosition - worldVertexPos.xyz);

  /* Compute the vector that comes from the camera. Because we
    are working in camera coordinates, camera is at origin so the
    calculation would be:
  normalize(vec3(0,0,0) - worldVertexPos.xyz); */
  vec3 viewVec = normalize(-worldVertexPos.xyz);

  /* Calculate the specular contribution. Reflect is a built-in
    function that returns the vector that is the reflection of
    a vector on a surface represented by its normal */
    vec3 reflectVec = reflect(-lightVec, normal);

  float spec = max(dot(reflectVec, viewVec), 0.0);
  spec = pow(spec, 16.0);
  vec4 specContrib = lightColor * spec;

  /* We don't want any ambient contribution, but
  let's write it down for teaching purposes */
  vec3 ambientContrib = vec3(0,0,0);
```

```
    // Calculate diffuse contribution
    vec3 diffContrib = lightColor * max(dot(lightVec, normal), 0);

    /* Final light contribution that will be interpolated in the
    fragment shader */
    lightContribution = ambientContrib + diffContrib + specContrib;
}

// fragment shader
#version 430
#pragma debug(on)
#pragma optimize(off)

// Interpolator for our light
smooth int vec3 lightContribution;

out vec4 frameBufferColor;

void main()
{
    frameBufferColor = vec4(lightContribution, 1.0);
}
```

This could seem a complex shader, but if you read it carefully, you can see that we didn't do anything really fancy: just addition/subtraction of some vectors, some normalization, and not much else.

This shader, also called per-vertex lighting, produces the following rendering:

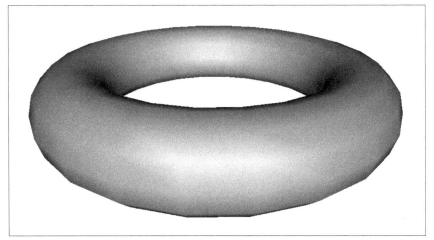

Gouraud lighting shader

Summary

In this chapter we learned how vertex shaders must be made and how to manage inputs and outputs. We also touched upon and understood a very important topic—the interpolators. Interpolators will be the basic mechanism of all our future shaders.

I also introduced some basic lighting concepts that, in the end, produced a per-vertex lit object. In the next chapter we will improve our lighting techniques, from per-fragment lighting to normal mapping. We will also see some other interesting imaging shaders.

4
Fragment Shaders

Fragment shaders are probably the most important type of shaders of all. They are so important that a casual reader would understand them simply as **shaders**.

Using fragment shaders is the only way of painting something on the screen. They are responsible for updating the framebuffer with colors and depth; so, in short, in the last term, all that you see on the screen is painted by a fragment shader.

In this chapter we will learn how fragment shaders are executed, what they can do, and what they can't. Also, we will see how fragment shaders interact with other pipeline stages.

Execution model

When a primitive stage has ended, its processing in the vertex primitive stages (vertex shaders, geometry shaders, and clipping) becomes rasterized. The fragment shader execution begins this rasterization.

Consider a triangle; in order to paint that triangle onto the screen you need to convert it from its native vectorial form (vertices coordinate) to discrete pixels. The system that carries out that action is the fragment shader module, being executed once per each fragment.

The more of the framebuffer's area the primitive covers, the more times the fragment shader will be executed. The fragment shaders' performance has direct influence on your application's **fill rate** (the speed at which the GPU can output fragments).

Having said that, let's see two very important constraints about fragment shaders:

- A fragment shader can't read the framebuffer. It's only capable of writing into it. If you need to mix your framebuffer with the result of your fragment shader computations, you only have two choices and both imply **multipass rendering techniques**:
    - Rely on the blending mechanism to mix the previous content of the framebuffer with your current rendering
    - Render firstly into a texture and use that texture as an input for your fragment shader
- A fragment shader is executed for a specific fragment that lies in a specific framebuffer location (x, y). In other words, you can't use your shader to modify other parts of the framebuffer.

Terminating a fragment shader

The usual way of terminating the execution of a fragment shader is when a `return` instruction is found or when the closing bracket of the `main` function is reached, but there is another one, especially for a fragment shader. If you use the keyword `discard`, the execution of the fragment shader at that point will stop, and the framebuffer won't be updated at all. This means that neither the color, depth, and stencil buffers, nor any other buffer that forms part of the framebuffer will be updated. Other subbuffers, such as the stencil buffer, for example, will also remain untouched. Think of discarding fragments as creating holes in your mesh.

Inputs and outputs

As the rest of the shaders, fragment shaders can receive uniform variables as input. They work exactly as for vertex shaders, so there isn't much to say at this point except if we talk about textures. Textures are represented by an opaque variable type: a sampler (an opaque type is a special type that can only be used with built-in functions and cannot be used in mathematical operations). To make a texture available, you have to declare its uniform variable, using the right sampler type. Depending on the class of the texture you should use one sampler or other. A brief list is:

- `sampler1D` (for 1D textures)
- `sampler2D` (for 2D textures)
- `sampler3D` (for 3D textures)

- samplerCube (for cubemaps)

- sampler2DArray (for arrays of 2D textures)

- sampler2DShadow (for 2D shadow maps)

Samplers are special variable types that can only be used as uniforms. You can't declare a sampler inside a function.

In the host application, when you want to upload a sampler you just have to upload a uniform integer type, representing the texture unit where the texture is currently bound. A common mistake is using the texture name (ID) instead of the texture unit. A little sample would be:

```
/* textureNames is an array of strings and ids with
name of the texture inside the shader */
for(int i = 0; i<numberOfTextures; ++i)
{
  // Activate texture unit 'i'
  glActiveTexture(GL_TEXTURE0 + i);
  glBindTexture(GL_TEXTURE_2D, textureNames[i].id);
  intloc = glGetUniformLocation(shaderID,
textureNames[i].name);
  glUniform1i(loc, i);
}
```

As said in *Chapter 3*, *Vertex Shaders*, fragment shaders receive vertex attributes (or other calculated values in a per-vertex basis) interpolated by one of the available manners (for us, linearly and perspective corrected); thanks to the interpolators.

Just to clarify, the term **interpolator** is not an official word in GLSL, but a description of what they do. Through different OpenGL versions, they had taken different names. In early GLSL versions and in the current OpenGL/ES Shading Language, their name is **varying** variables. Currently, in OpenGL, there are simply the in variables, but because in is not a very good name and varying is outdated, I'll refer to them as interpolators.

As outputs, I will mention two. During a fragment shader execution you must output the current fragment's color. This is mandatory and the main duty of a fragment shader, but you optionally can modify the fragment's depth.

In order to modify the fragment's depth, you don't need to declare anything, because a special built-in variable already exists for that purpose: gl_FragDepth. Writing to that variable (it's just a float variable) will modify the fragment's depth. This is very handy for some effects like HUDs, 3D font rendering, coronas, sun flares, and so on, but not for normal renderings, so we will rarely modify it in the examples.

Examples

In the following pages I'm going to present some examples, from the most basic one to a complex lighting shader.

Solid color mesh

The first one is a very simple shader that writes the mesh in a solid color, received using a uniform variable:

```
#version 430
#debug(on)
#optimize(off)
uniform vec4 SolidColor;
out vec4 FBColor;

void main()
{
  FBColor= SolidColor;
}
```

Using a half red color stored in the `SolidColor` uniform variable, over a cylinder mesh, we get the following rendering:

Using only uniforms as input we can't do much more than this, so I'll colorize the cylinder using its own vertices' positions.

Interpolated colored mesh

First, in the vertex shader, set up an interpolator of vec3 type and place the xyz of the position attribute there. Then, use the following fragment shader:

```
#version 430
#pragma debug(on)
#pragma optimize(off)

uniform vec4 SolidColor;
in vec3 InterpolatedPosition;

out vec4 FBColor;
void main()
{
   FBColor = vec4(InterpolatedPosition, 1.0);
}
```

The following is the vertex colorized cylinder as result of rendering with this last shader:

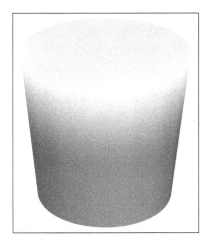

Before explaining this example, let me explain a bit about colors in fragment shaders. Colors are represented in the range 0 to 1, where 0 is the minimum intensity and 1 is the maximum intensity. The values in between represent intermediate intensities. A complete color is composed with four channels: red, green, blue, and alpha (transparency) in the respective order. For example, (1, 0, 0, 1) represents opaque pure red, (1, 1, 0, 1) is opaque pure yellow, (0.5, 0.5, 0.5, 0.5) is semi-transparent grey.

Perhaps you worked in the past with colors in the range 0 to 255. It's the same thing, and the only difference is that inside a shader, colors are automatically normalized, and more importantly, they are clamped. So, if because of a calculation, a color becomes -1.5 or 2.9, it is clamped to 0 or 1.

Having said that, let's see what happened to our cylinder. Because the vertex coordinates are in an arbitrary range, probably larger than 1 and with negative values, they are clamped to [0,1], which means that any vertex value larger than 1 will be saturated when used as a color, and given that the cylinder is centered in (0,0,0), colors are kind of radial. So, because in our sample RGB is in the same order as XYZ, R represents the x direction, G the y direction, and B the z direction, and that explains why our cylinder takes those colors.

Now that you have a rough idea of what things we can achieve with the available elements, we will unlock the full potential of fragment shaders with the use of textures.

Using interpolators to compute the texture coordinates

Using the vertex shader of the previous chapter that enabled an interpolator for texture coordinates, we are going to map a texture onto our cylinder using the following fragment shader:

```
#version 430
#pragma debug(on)
#pragma optimize(off)

uniform sampler2D Image;
in vec2 TexCoordInterpolated;

out vec4 FBColor;
void main()
{
  /* Next line means: "take the texel (texture pixel) of
  'Image' at 'TexCoordInterpolated' position" */
  FBColor = texture(Image, TexCoordInterpolated);
}
```

As you can see I've used a built-in function; in this case, `texture`. There are many texture lookup functions, depending on the usage we pretend. You can read about them in the GLSL specification, but we will focus only on normal texture lookup functions such as `texture`.

Also, I declared an identifier for the texture. This is a sampler type variable and it can only be used in texture lookup functions.

Our textured models would look like the following rendering:

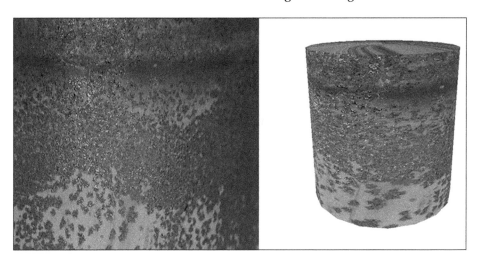

Phong lighting

It's time now for a more complex shader. I'm going to continue with the lighting shader shown in the *Chapter 3, Vertex Shaders*, but this time, I'll pass all calculations to the fragment shader.

The goal of the next shader will be to achieve per-pixel lighting, but using a mask stored in the alpha channel of the texture to nullify the light's specular contribution on those red rusty areas.

In addition, I'm going to use a more detailed 3D model. The most common purpose of adding lighting to a 3D scene is to empathize the surface's details. A plane or a cylinder has no surface details because they are uniform so no details will be improved by the use of lighting there.

So, let's start out with a sample of the Phong shading:

```
// Vertex shader for simple Phongs Lighting model
#version 430
#pragma optimize(off)
#pragma debug(on)

uniform mat4 Modelview;
uniform mat4 Projection;

/* Matrix to transform normals. This is the transpose of the
   inverse of the upper leftmost 3x3 of the modelview matrix */
uniform mat3 NormalMatrix;

layout (location = 0) in vec3 Position;
layout (location = 1) in vec2 TextCoord;
layout (location = 2) in vec3 Normal;

smooth out vec2 TextCoordInterp;
smooth out vec3 PositionInterp;

/*This time we will interpolate the Normal, not the total computed
lighting contribution*/
smooth out vec3 NormalInterp;

void main()
{
    PositionInterp = (Modelview * vec4(Position, 1.0)).xyz;
    TextCoordInterp = TextCoord;

    // Normals transform
    NormalInterp = normalize(NormalMatrix * Normal);
    gl_Position = Projection * Modelview * vec4(Position, 1.0);
}
```

The only difference with the shader explained in the previous chapter is that we are, additionally, interpolating the vertex position. This interpolated value, in the fragment shader will be the effective 3D position in camera coordinates (because we transformed it using the modelview matrix) of each triangle's fragment. We need this value because we are going to compute the lighting at that exact point:

```
// fragment shader for simple Phongs Lighting model
#version 430
#pragma optimize(off)
#pragma debug(on)
```

```glsl
uniform sampler2D Image;

// Light position, in camera coordinates
uniform vec3 LightPosition;

// The color of our light
uniform vec3 LightColor;
smooth in vec2 TextCoordInterp;
smooth in vec3 NormalInterp;
smooth in vec3 PositionInterp;

out vec4 FBColor;

void main()
{
    /* After interpolation, normals probably are denormalized,
    so we need renormalize them */
    vec3 normal = normalize(NormalInterp);

    /*Calculate the rest of parameters exactly like we did in the
vertex shader version of this shader*/
vec3 lightVec = normalize(LightPosition - PositionInterp);
vec3 viewVec = normalize(-PositionInterp);
vec3 reflectVec = reflect(-lightVec, normal);
float spec = max(dot(reflectVec, viewVec), 0.0);
spec = pow(spec, 16.0);
vec4 textureColor = texture(Image, TextCoordInterp);

vec3 specContrib = LightColor * spec;

 // No ambient contribution this time
vec3 ambientContrib = vec3(0.0, 0.0, 0.0);

vec3 diffContrib = LightColor * max(dot(lightVec, normal), 0.0);

/* Apply the mask to the specular contribution. The "1.0 -" is
To invert the texture's alpha channel */
vec3 lightContribution = ambientContrib + diffContrib + (specContrib *
(1.0 - textureColor.a));

FBColor = vec4(textureColor.rgb * lightContribution, 1.0);
}
```

As you can see, the shader is 90 percent equal to the per-vertex light version, but the resulting rendering differs quite a lot.

 Remember that normalizing the normal vector again in the fragment shader, because after the interpolation, it will be denormalized. Also, all other vectors must be normalized too. This is very important, because the dot products involved in the calculations need the normalized values to work correctly.

I'll show a few variants of this shader to see what is happening inside when lighting, texture, and masks are progressively applied.

First, let's view the result when no lighting is applied at all, and only texturing is applied:

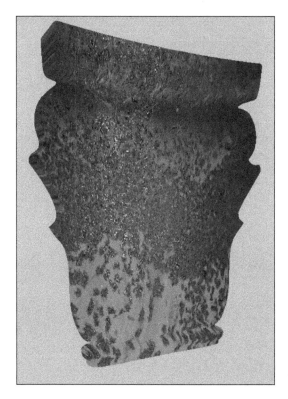

It's not very detailed, isn't it? Well, let's see what happens when we replace the texture by the lighting calculations, using the same exact mesh:

This has more appeal, doesn't it? Notice the specular reflections, the brightest ones, and the smooth darkening in the areas where the light barely reaches.

To achieve this lighting effect, go to the fragment shader and just remove the texture lookup and replace the two last lines with the following:

```
vec3 lightContribution = ambientContrib + diffContrib + specContrib;
FBColor = vec4(vec3(lightContribution), 1.0);
```

Now, let's see how the mask stored in the alpha channel hides the specular contribution in the next render:

If you want this result, just multiply the specular contribution by one minus the alpha channel of the texture (*1.0 - textureColor.a*).

Now, let's combine the lighting with the mask and the texture, which is the exact result of the shader I explained earlier:

Notice here how the red dusty areas obscure the specular contribution, making this model more realistic.

Nowadays, **Phong** is a basic lighting model, but some years ago (not many!) it was an advanced model, because graphics cards only had enough processing power for this. Now, shaders could be bigger and more complex, and even they could have nested loops, or loops with a variable iterations number (coming from a uniform variable or textures) rather than fixed ones. They can have branches, functions, tens of texture accesses, and many other things.

These days one could program a ray tracer inside a shader or even another Global Illumination Lighting Model such as Ambient Occlusion or Radiosity. The power is there for you to use.

Summary

In this chapter we learnt about how to complete the pipeline in order to write shader programs that effectively produce a complete and valid output.

We also learned the techniques needed to render from the most basic algorithm, a solid color, and a complete illumination model (Phong). You should be able to face any other rendering type, mixing textures with calculations to produce awesome results.

You now have the tools to build advanced effects by yourself, such as normal mapping, reflections, parallax, and post-processing.

In the next chapter we will face a different type of shader, not meant to define the final aspect to our scene but to provide more flexibility and complexity.

5
Geometry Shaders

Up until now, we've learnt the basic configuration of the pipeline and how to produce a render using a soup of triangles and textures. In this chapter, we will add a new shader type to our knowledge set. It will serve to improve our scenes, giving them more flexibility by letting us interact more deeply with the pipeline, but without having to increase the CPU side code or the bandwidth between the CPU and the GPU.

In this chapter, we will learn how these new shaders work and cover a few examples of techniques where geometry shaders could give us great flexibility. We will cover the following topics:

- How to replicate geometry on the fly, for example, to make twin models
- How to make a particle or crowd system with complex-shaped particles parting from bare points

Geometry shaders versus vertex shaders

Although geometry shaders transform vertices in a very similar way than vertex shaders do, we have to enumerate some important differences between them:

- Vertex shaders are executed once by an incoming vertex. Geometry shaders are executed once (by default) by an incoming primitive.
- Vertex shaders can't access any information about adjacent vertices. A geometry shader has all the information for a given primitive and adjacent ones.
- Vertex shaders don't produce new vertices. Geometry shaders create new primitives (in fact, that's the main purpose).

In addition, there are other facts about geometry shaders that must be known:

- The geometry shader stage happens after the primitive assembly stage.

- A geometry shader receives assembled primitives. This means that it doesn't matter if you send triangles, triangle strips, or fans of triangles. A geometry shader will always receive a triangle. The same happens with lines, line strips, or line loops. The primitives that will reach the geometry shader will be single lines.

- The incoming primitive will be discarded after geometry shader execution.

- The type of the input primitive isn't forced to be the output. This means that, for example, we can use points as inputs and triangle strips as outputs.

Geometry shaders are available as an OpenGL extension from almost any OpenGL version, but since Version 4.0, a geometry shader can be invoked more than once per primitive. You can use a built-in variable (`gl_InvocationID`) to distinguish between each execution on the same primitive during the same draw call.

There are also a lot of additional outputs for a geometry shader rather than the primitives (viewport ID, layer ID), but these are meant for advanced users and we will not care much about them.

Inputs and outputs

Besides the usual inputs and outputs (uniforms and vertex attributes), there are new elements that need to be considered.

Primitives, our main input and output element, are complex, and because of that we have to be careful and specify very well what we are doing at each time. The primitive type specified in the geometry shader must match exactly with the primitive that we are drawing (using a GL call like `glDrawArrays`, for instance). This means that we cannot happily write a general purpose geometry shader for everything. Also, we have to specify the primitive type and the number of vertices that will be emitted (created) statically in the shader.

For these purposes, we have the `layout` keyword. With it, we could define an input and an output layout. As an example, we could do something similar to the following:

```
layout(triangles) in;
layout(triangle_strip, max_vertices = 6) out;
```

Options for an input layout are as follows:

- `points`
- `lines` (this includes primitives drawn as `GL_LINES`, `GL_LINE_STRIP`, and `GL_LINE_LOOP`)
- `lines_adjacency` (`GL_LINES_ADJACENCY GL_LINE_STRIP_ADJACENCY`)
- `triangles` (including `GL_TRIANGLES`, and `GL_TRIANGLE_STRIP`, and `GL_TRIANGLE_FAN`)
- `triangles_adjacency` (including `GL_TRIANGLES_ADJACENCY` and `GL_TRIANGLE_STRIP_ADJACENCY`)

Options for an output layer are as follows:

- `points`
- `line_strip`
- `triangle_strip`

> Note that in case of single triangles, single lines cannot be used as output. If you want to output more than one line or more than one triangle, it must be in both cases, in the form of strips. Also, input and output types are not related, as we will see in the examples of this chapter.

Also, you must specify statically the number of vertices that will be emitted (`max_vertices`).

Interface blocks

With the incorporation of a new type of shaders, communications between all of them becomes a little complex. Now it isn't enough with basic interpolators (although the basic concept is still there). A new mechanism called **interface blocks** handles this communication in a more efficient way.

Think of an interface block as structures (although they really aren't) that serve to interconnect shaders' stages. Interface block definitions must match in the shaders they are declared in, if not, a linkage error will occur.

At this point, we have two in-between spaces: between the vertex and geometry shaders and between the geometry and fragment shaders. For the first case, we have to define an output interface block in the vertex shader, and the same interface block in the geometry shader but as an input block. Let's give an example:

```
// vertex shader output interface block
out MyPerVertexVariables
{
  smooth vec2 TextCoords;
  smooth vec3 Normal;
} perVertex;
// geometry shader input interface block
in MyPerVertexVariables
{
  smooth vec2 TextCoords;
  smooth vec3 Normal;
} perVertex[]; // here the instance name is an array, to hold all
perVertex of a primitive
```

In the case of the communication between geometry and fragment shaders, it's more or less the same:

```
// Geometry shader output interface block
out MyInterpolators
{
  smooth vec2 TextCoords;
  smooth vec3 Normal;
}interpolators;
// fragment shader input interface block
in MyInterpolators
{
  smooth vec2 TextCoords;
  smooth vec3 Normal;
}interpolators;
```

As you can see, this is more or less the same as using normal in/out variables, but there are some logic restrictions (a fragment shader can't define an output interface block, a vertex shader can't define an input interface block).

The key to allow GLSL to perform the linkage between two interface blocks is that the struct name (not the variable!) must be the same. In our example, MyInterpolators, MyPerVertexVariables, and the fields defined inside must match exactly in the two involved shader stages.

The interface block's variable name doesn't affect the linkage. It can be different in both blocks.

Also, GLSL provides us with a built-in interface block called `gl_in`. It is intended for holding a primitive's vertices positions, and it has been defined in this way:

```
in gl_PerVertex
{
    vec4 gl_Position;
    float gl_PointSize;
    float gl_ClipDistance[];
} gl_in[];
```

The variables `gl_PointSize` and `gl_ClipDistance` don't have much interest for us right now. We will focus on `gl_Position`.

To give an example, consider that our input types are `triangles`, then `gl_in` will have a size of 3 (one element per vertex) and each `gl_in[].gl_Position` will be the position of that vertex after being transformed by the vertex shader and assembled during the primitive assembly stage.

A last note about interface blocks is that they can be unnamed. You are not forced to give them an instance (variable) name. If you choose this manner, the access to the members is just the member name. In a vertex, `shaders gl_Position` is implicitly declared as:

```
out gl_PerVertex
{
    vec4 gl_Position;
    float gl_PointSize;
    float gl_ClipDistance[];
};
```

As the preceding interface block has no instance name, you can safely access the members directly, as you were doing until now. You can also do this with your own interface blocks, but for the sake of code clarity, I'd suggest to use them with the usual structure's nomenclature (name of the structure dot member)

Example – pass-thru shader

Let's write our first geometry shader, a pass-thru shader that will produce as output the same primitive that reaches the geometry shader as input:

```
#version 430
#pragma optimize(off)
```

```
#pragma debug(on)
// Establish our primitive's input and output types, as well as the
number of vertices that we will produce.
layout(triangles) in;
layout(triangle_strip, max_vertices = 3) out;
void main()
{
  // GLSL provides us with the .length() method for arrays. It tells
us the number of elements in the vector.
    for(int i = 0; i < gl_in.length(); ++i)
    {
    // gl_in is the standard input interface block
        gl_Position = gl_in[i].gl_Position;
        // The next function, will emit the computed vertex to the
pipeline
        EmitVertex();
    }
// The next function will close the primitive
    EndPrimitive();
}
```

The pass-thru shader has no effect in the sense as the rendering is not affected at all. It is not very useful in a real environment, but it is very handy to show how a new primitive is produced.

Creating a new primitive is as simple as writing out all out variables of a vertex (in this case, only gl_Position) and then calling the function EmitVertex(). This function will effectively create a new vertex with the data that has been filled in the out variables. When you are done with all vertices, a simple call to the EndPrimitive() function will close the primitive and make it ready for further pipeline stages.

Example – using attributes in the interface blocks

For the next example, we will need to use more vertex attributes than the position, so we will have to create an interface block to pass all of them to the geometry shader.

Let's see this in the following example:

```
// Vertex shader
#version 430
#pragma optimize(off)
#pragma debug(on)
uniform mat4 Modelview;
```

```
uniform mat4 Projection;
layout (location = 0) in vec3 Position;
layout (location = 1) in vec2 TextCoord;
layout (location = 2) in vec3 Normal;
// Now, we will define in this block the interpolators
out VertexData
{
    smooth vec2 TextCoord;
    smooth vec3 Normal;
} vertexOut;
void main()
{
    gl_Position = Projection * Modelview * vec4(Position, 1.0);
    vertexOut.TextCoord = TextCoord;
    vertexOut.Normal = Normal;
}
```

Now, in the geometry shader, we will catch these new values using the block in an array style:

```
#version 430
#pragma optimize(off)
#pragma debug(on)
layout(triangles) in;
layout(triangle_strip, max_vertices = 3) out;
// The important point here is "VertexData". It must match with the
vertex shader version.
// input interface block, from the vertex shader
in VertexData
{
    smooth vec2 TextCoord;
    smooth vec3 Normal;
} vertexIn[]; // The name of the variable doesn't have to match with
the vertex shader's version
// Output interface block, going to the fragment shader
out Interpolators
{
    smooth vec2 TextCoord;
    smooth vec3 Normal;
}interpolators;

void main()
{
    for(int i = 0; i < gl_in.length(); ++i)
    {
```

```
        gl_Position = gl_in[i].gl_Position;
        interpolators.TextCoord = vertexIn[i].TextCoord;
        interpolators.Normal = vertexIn[i].Normal;
        EmitVertex();
    }
    EndPrimitive();
}
```

> Remember, all output variables and interface blocks defined in a geometry shader are per vertex.

In the fragment shader, we catch the interpolated values as always:

```
#version 430
#pragma optimize(off)
#pragma debug(on)
uniform sampler2D Image;
// From geometry shader or from vertex shader
in Interpolators
{
    smooth vec2 TextCoord;
    smooth vec3 Normal;
}interpData;
out vec4 FBColor;
void main()
{
    vec4 textureColor = texture2D(Image, interpData.TextCoord);
    // do something with interpData.normal;
    FBColor = vec4(textureColor.rgb, 1.0);
}
```

Now we have all the basic mechanisms in our hands that we will need to write a full featured geometry shader, so let's go with a shader that will make this type of shader interesting.

A crowd of butterflies

In this example, we are going to see how to render complex structures, creating all information on the fly.

Our aim is to render a crowd of butterflies using the CPU as less as possible by performing calculations (transforms, flag aperture, butterfly's yaw/pitch, and so on). We will start from a random distribution of points in the space. No vertex attributes other than the points position will be used, and from them, we will create for each point two textured rectangles (triangle strips), one for each of a butterfly's wings. We will also change the wings' apertures and butterflies' flying directions using distinct values based on the `gl_PrimitiveID` built-in variable (we will cover more on this variable later).

To summarize the way we are going to build these triangle strips from a single point, a picture is worth a thousand words:

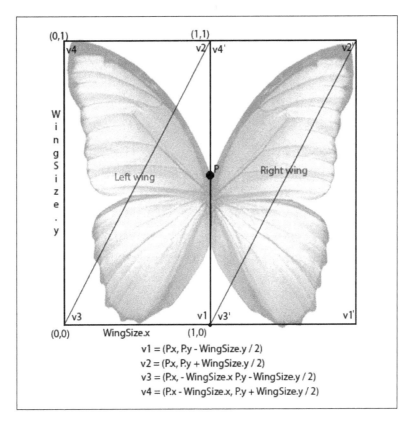

$$v1 = (P.x, P.y - WingSize.y / 2)$$
$$v2 = (P.x, P.y + WingSize.y / 2)$$
$$v3 = (P.x, - WingSize.x P.y - WingSize.y / 2)$$
$$v4 = (P.x - WingSize.x, P.y + WingSize.y / 2)$$

With P, the original point size, we compute the corners of both triangle strips by adding or subtracting the wing dimensions that we are passing as a uniform variable.

Now, let's get started with the code:

1. First, let's write our vertex shader, which, by the way, is the most simple vertex shader we could ever write:

    ```
    #version 430
    #pragma optimize(off)
    #pragma debug(on)
    layout (location = 0) in vec3 Position;
    void main()
    {
        /* This time we won't transform the position here,
        but in the Geometry Shader*/
        gl_Position = vec4(Position, 1.0);
    }
    ```

2. Now, to put all simple things together, let's see the fragment shader, which isn't very involved either:

    ```
    #version 430
    #pragma optimize(off)
    #pragma debug(on)
    uniform sampler2D Image;
    // Interface block to pass the texture coordinates to the fragment
    shader
    in Interpolators
    {
        smooth vec2 TextCoord;
    }interpData;

    out vec4 FBColor;
    void main()
    {
        vec4 textureColor = texture2D(Image, interpData.TextCoord);
         /* To render only the parts where the texture is not
           transparent, we discard those fragments who are
           transparent in some degree */
        if(textureColor.a < 0.4)
        {
            discard;
        }
        FBColor = textureColor;
    }
    ```

3. Now, let's go with the core of our program, the geometry shader:

```glsl
#version 430
#pragma optimize(off)
#pragma debug(on)
layout(points) in; // we feed the GS with points
/* The output will be two separated triangle strips, 4 vertices
each one. We will rotate each triangle strip using the shared edge
as pivot */
layout(triangle_strip, max_vertices = 8) out;
uniform vec2 WingSize;
uniform int NumberOfPrimitives; // total number of points
uniform mat4 Modelview;
uniform mat4 Projection;
out Interpolators
{
    smooth vec2 TextCoord;
}interpData;
void main()
{
    /* Alpha angle is the wings aperture angle. This will give us
       a rotation in the range [5, 85] degrees */
    // gl_PrimitiveIDIn is the index of the current primitive
    that is being processed.
    float alpha = radians(5.0f + (gl_PrimitiveIDIn /
    (NumberOfPrimitives - 1.0f)) * 80.0);
    // Beta angle is the orientation of the butterfly
    float beta = radians(-90.0f + (gl_PrimitiveIDIn /
    (NumberOfPrimitives - 1.0f)) * 90.0f);
    // Matrix to translate the wing to the origin
    mat4 T = mat4(vec4(1,0,0,0),
                  vec4(0,1,0,0),
                  vec4(0,0,1,0),
                  vec4(-gl_in[0].gl_Position.xyz,1));

    // Matrix to translate the wing back to its original position
    mat4 Ti = mat4(vec4(1,0,0,0),
                   vec4(0,1,0,0),
                   vec4(0,0,1,0),
                   vec4(gl_in[0].gl_Position.xyz,1));
    /* Matrix to rotate the whole butterfly to change its flying
       direction. This is a Z axis rotation matrix. */
    mat4 Rz = mat4(vec4(cos(beta),  sin(beta),  0, 0),
                   vec4(-sin(beta), cos(beta),  0, 0),
                   vec4(0,          0,          1, 0),
```

```
                         vec4(0,              0,              0, 1));
        // Left wing creation.
        // Matrix to rotate the left wing and give an appearance of
        moving wings. This is a Y axis rotation matrix
        mat4 Ry = mat4(vec4(cos(alpha),    0,    -sin(alpha),    0),
                       vec4(0,             1,    0,              0),
                       vec4(sin(alpha),    0,    cos(alpha),     0),
                       vec4(0,             0,    0,              1));
        // Final transform matrix
        mat4 M = Projection * Modelview * Rz * Ti * Ry * T;
```

4. Until now, we have only prepared the matrices to perform the rotations in the way the next diagram shows.

5. The butterfly positioning and wings aperture diagram that you get is as follows:

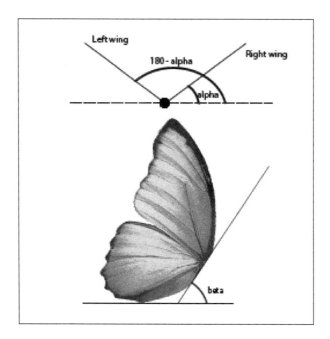

6. Now, let's compute the vertices. The process is very straightforward. Just compute the positions and the other vertex attributes and emit that vertex. When you are done with all the primitive's vertices, finish it with EndPrimitive():

   ```
   // Using the original point's position and the wing's size,
   we calculate each new vertex. Then we transform it with the
   accumulated matrix (M)
   ```

```
gl_Position = M * vec4(gl_in[0].gl_Position.x, gl_in[0].
gl_Position.y - WingSize.y / 2.0f, gl_in[0].gl_Position.zw);
// Create a proper texture coordinate for this vertex
interpData.TextCoord = vec2(1.0f, 0.0f);
EmitVertex();
// 2nd vertex
gl_Position = M * vec4(gl_in[0].gl_Position.x, gl_in[0].
gl_Position.y + WingSize.y / 2.0f, gl_in[0].gl_Position.zw);
interpData.TextCoord = vec2(1.0f, 1.0f);
EmitVertex();

// 3rd vertex
gl_Position = M * vec4(gl_in[0].gl_Position.x - WingSize.x,
gl_in[0].gl_Position.y - WingSize.y / 2.0f, gl_in[0].
gl_Position.zw);
interpData.TextCoord = vec2(0.0f, 0.0f);
EmitVertex();
//4rd vertex
gl_Position = M * vec4(gl_in[0].gl_Position.x - WingSize.x,
gl_in[0].gl_Position.y + WingSize.y / 2.0f, gl_in[0].
gl_Position.zw);
interpData.TextCoord = vec2(0.0f, 1.0f);
EmitVertex();
EndPrimitive();
```

7. Here we are done with the left wing. Now, because the right wing has an opposite rotation, we need to compute a new rotation matrix and a new accumulated transform matrix:

```
// The aperture angle for the right wing is 180 - alpha
alpha = 3.141592f - alpha;
Ry = mat4(vec4(cos(alpha),  0, -sin(alpha), 0),
          vec4(0,           1, 0,           0),
          vec4(sin(alpha),  0, cos(alpha),  0),
          vec4(0,           0, 0,           1));
M = Projection * Modelview * Rz * Ti * Ry * T;
gl_Position = M * vec4(gl_in[0].gl_Position.x + WingSize.x,
gl_in[0].gl_Position.y - WingSize.y / 2.0f, gl_in[0].
gl_Position.zw);
interpData.TextCoord = vec2(0.0f, 0.0f);
EmitVertex();
gl_Position = M * vec4(gl_in[0].gl_Position.x + WingSize.x,
gl_in[0].gl_Position.y + WingSize.y / 2.0f, gl_in[0].
gl_Position.zw);
interpData.TextCoord = vec2(0.0f, 1.0f);
EmitVertex();
```

```
        gl_Position = M * vec4(gl_in[0].gl_Position.x, gl_in[0].
        gl_Position.y - WingSize.y / 2.0f, gl_in[0].gl_Position.zw);
        interpData.TextCoord = vec2(1.0f, 0.0f);
        EmitVertex();
        gl_Position = M * vec4(gl_in[0].gl_Position.x, gl_in[0].
        gl_Position.y + WingSize.y / 2.0f, gl_in[0].gl_Position.zw);
        interpData.TextCoord = vec2(1.0f, 1.0f);
        EmitVertex();
        EndPrimitive();
    }
```

This was a long shader, but if you read it, the most complicated things are the transforms. The rest, creating and filling vertex attributes, is quite simple.

Now, as a reward, this is the final output of this shader:

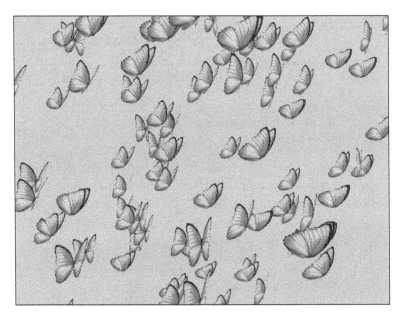

Summary

In this chapter, we have learnt how to use the GPU to offload the CPU in some rendering tasks. The butterflies example taught us how, parting from a plain array of 3D points, we can create on the fly more elaborated (in terms of mesh complexity) structures using only the GPU. A good exercise for you would be to give life to the butterflies by animating their wings (easy to achieve, changing the wings' aperture angle according to the time), coloring each butterfly instance differently based on `gl_PrimitiveID`, or calculating the strips' normal vectors to include lighting calculations.

In the next chapter, we will increase the flexibility of our renders with the usage of the compute shaders, which will allow us to perform other GPU calculations without being constrained by the pipeline's execution order.

6
Compute Shaders

Up to this point, we have followed the rendering pipeline rules. Data was always sent in the form of vertex buffers or textures and was transformed accordingly with very well defined steps. Now we will learn about a new mechanism to use the GPU in a more flexible way with all the advantages of GLSL. This means that, as opposed to the other GPU solutions, we will have all the available OpenGL texture formats (not a restricted subset like in CUDA or OpenCL), vector and matrix types, and built-in functions.

Compute shaders is a quite extensive topic, with a lot of details that cannot be covered in a single chapter of any book. It is for that reason that in this chapter, we will cover only the basics, a brief introduction of the compute shaders' language, and the possibilities that they could bring to us.

In this chapter, we will learn how generic GPU processes are arranged into the processor and how they are executed. We will not only focus on rendering and image modifications, but also on producing numerical results too.

Execution model

In the case of different shader types, the **Rendering Pipeline** decided how and when they had to be invoked. Since the Rendering Pipeline stopped working, we had to take care of its jobs—synchronization, thread management, and so on.

Anticipate a single computer shader execution. Computer shaders' terminology defines this as a work item. These work items cannot be invoked independently; they are separated in groups. A work group encapsulates an arbitrary number of work items, which is specified by the programmer but limited by the hardware capabilities. Work groups run all their items in a parallel way—more or less synchronized. Also, items inside a group can share memory and synchronization mechanisms. All work groups must have the same number of work items and each work group is executed independently from the others, totally isolated, and in an unspecified order.

Furthermore, work groups are grouped by dimensions. We can choose to arrange them in one, two, or three dimensions.

The setup of the work items and work groups is split between the host application and the shaders' source code. In the host application, during the GL call that invokes the compute shader, we'll specify how many work groups we are going to use, and in the shader's source code, we'll define how many work items will compose a work group.

The dimensionality of work groups is meant to help us to index our problem. You would think that the more work groups and work items, the better, because that way we use more parts of the GPU and that will render in more performance. That is correct, but performance isn't everything. Although the same number of work items will be executed configuring ten work groups with ten work items (10 x 10 = 100) rather than if we configure five work groups in x dimension and two work groups in y dimension, with ten work items per group (5 x 2 x 10 = 100), the index of the work item being executed could help us a lot depending on how the problem is structured. It is like processing a whole image accessing the pixels in a one-dimensional way versus using x and y to access the pixels.

From the shader, we can access some very useful information: the work group where the current work item is in, the ID of the current work item inside a work group, the global work item ID (work item ID multiplied by the work group size), and, few more. These IDs will help us to index arrays, images (or even arrays of images!), and buffers of one, two, and three dimensions. The built-in variables that are available in the language for helping us to manage and arrange those IDs are the following:

```
// Total number of work groups in each dimension
in uvec3 gl_NumWorkGroups;
// Number of work items inside a work group
const uvec3 gl_WorkGroupSize;
// Index of the work group that is currently in execution
in uvec3 gl_WorkGroupID;
// Index of the work item (inside a work group) that is currently in
execution
in uvec3 gl_LocalInvocationID;
/* Global index of the current work item (gl_WorkGroupID *
   gl_WorkGroupSize + gl_LocalInvocationID;) */
in uvec3 gl_GlobalInvocationID;
/*
This is a one dimensional representation of gl_LocalInvocationID (gl_
LocalInvocationID.z * gl_WorkGroupSize.x * gl_WorkGroupSize.y
    + gl_LocalInvocationID.y * gl_WorkGroupSize.x +
    gl_LocalInvocationID.x;)
*/
uint gl_LocalInvocationIndex;
```

But, if instead of traversing a one-dimensional array we have to traverse an image, we can arrange work items and work groups to use them to index both dimensions of the image, and that way set or get a pixel of the image. For instance, if we have an image with a size of 512 x 512, we can say that we are going to use work groups of 32 items in x and 32 items in y, and use 16 work groups in x and the other 16 in y (32 x 16 = 512).

The number of available work items and work groups is limited by the hardware. You can ask OpenGL in the host application for those limits.

Render to texture example

The first example will take a texture and will write into it some colors. To illustrate the use of work groups and work items, we will paint each pixel of the image with the index of the work group that processes that pixel. As we will use 16 x 16 work groups, the image will be filled with 16 x 16 solid block colors.

The shader invocation is done with this line: glDispatchCompute(16, 16, 1);. That means that we are going to execute the shader with 16 work groups in the x and y dimensions and 1 in the z (1 is the minimum accepted value for a dimension).

```
#version 430
// Configure how many work items compose the work groups
// Because we are executing the shader with 16 x 16 work groups, we
can handle images is 512 x 512 (16*32)
layout(local_size_x = 32,local_size_y = 32, local_size_z = 1) in;
// Declare the uniform variable that holds our image
uniform layout(rgba8) writeonly image2D Image;
void main()
{
   ivec2 position = ivec2(gl_GlobalInvocationID.xy);
   vec4 color=vec4(gl_WorkGroupID / vec3(gl_NumWorkGroups), 1.0);
   imageStore(Image, position, color);
}
```

There are some things to notice in the preceding few lines.

First, you can see that we configure the work item. Also, you can see new keywords in the uniform sampler declaration (we will address this later).

Most importantly, we use the global ID (if we enumerate all work items linearly, the global ID would be that of the index) of the current work item. In this case, these values go from 0 to 511 on each dimension (16 work groups x 32 work items = 512 shader executions), but the most important thing is the next line: to access the image, we are using a new texture access function (imageStore) that takes integral values, ranged from 0 to texture size 1. This is very different than in regular shaders, where texture coordinates were floating point variables and the values were normalized. This is done in this way in compute shaders in part to avoid any kind of filterings, roundings, or inaccuracies at the moment of writing into a texture. We have to specify the exact texel that we are going to access.

As promised, this shader produced a 16 x 16 blocky figure, like this one:

About the last example: in compute shaders, when you deal with images, you have to handle them in a different way than you do with vertex, fragment, or geometry shaders.

The image's access mode and format have to be set up according to the following table:

Float image formats	Integer image formats	Unsigned int image formats
rgba32f	rgba32i	rgba32ui
rgba16f	rgba16i	rgba16ui
rg32f	rgba8i	rgb10_a2ui
rg16f	rg32i	rgba8ui
r11f_g11f_b10f	rg16i	rg32ui
r32f	rg8i	rg16ui
r16f	r32i	rg8ui
rgba16	r16i	r32ui
rgb10_a2	r8i	r16ui
rgba8		r8ui
rg16		
rg8		
r16		
r8		
rgba16_snorm		
rgba8_snorm		
rg16_snorm		
rg8_snorm		
r16_snorm		
r8_snorm		

As you have read in this line in the last example, `uniform layout(rgba8) writeonly image2D Image;`, we have used the layout qualifier enclosing the image format. This line also specifies the access mode.

> In order to bind a texture in the host application, we cannot use the `glBindTexture` function as usual. We have to use a new function: `glBindImageTexture(0, texID, 0, GL_FALSE, 0, GL_WRITE_ ONLY, GL_RGBA8);`. The last two parameters must match with the texture declaration inside the compute shaders.

The last thing we will cover regarding compute shaders that handle texture images is synchronization. Compute shader execution is asynchronous, so the `glDispatchCompute` function will return as soon as it sends the information to the GPU. It won't wait for the compute shader to finish, so it may happen that if you execute two compute shaders that overlap in time and one of the shaders writes into the image, the other shader may read incorrect values, so it's common to force the shader that writes into the image to finish before executing the other that reads from the same image. This is done with one of the synchronization functions provided by OpenGL in the host application part: `glMemoryBarrier(GL_SHADER_IMAGE_ACCESS_BARRIER_BIT);`. Just call it immediately after the `glDispatchCompute` function to block further executions until the shader has finished its job.

Raw data computations

The following sample code is another very simple compute shader example, but it completes the basic sets of operations. First, we handled image data, now, we will handle raw data. In this example, the shader will receive two arrays of the same size, and we will use the shader to sum them together into a third array.

As always, let's go first with the shader's code:

```
#version 430
layout (local_size_x = 16, local_size_y = 1, local_size_z = 1) in;
uniform int BufferSize;
layout(std430, binding = 0) buffer InputBufferA{float inA[];};
layout(std430, binding = 1) buffer InputBufferB{float inB[];};
layout(std430, binding=2) buffer OutputBuffer{float outBuffer[];};
void main()
{
  uint index = gl_GlobalInvocationID.x;
  if(index >= BufferSize)
  {
    return;
  }
  outBuffer[index] = inA[index] + inB[index];
}
```

As you can see, we are using each work item to process only one array's element. The two important things here are the declaration of the buffers and the return that controls the access to our buffers.

The first thing to notice is that, the declaration of the array contains some elements. As seen in previous chapters, they are like an interface block declaration with some particularities. Let's inspect the first buffer declaration:

- The term `InputBufferA` is the name of the interface block. It isn't used in the code.

- The `float inA[];` global array declares an array of floats, and the variable that will hold them is `inA`.

- The `buffer` keyword denotes the type of the interface block.

- The `binding = 0` declaration denotes that this buffer corresponds to the one that was linked to the binding point `0` in the host application.

The `std430` storage qualifier is a memory layout qualifier. It contains information about the offset and alignment of the structure members (if the buffer is a buffer of structures). It is meant to be used with the shader interface blocks (buffer inputs for computer shaders). On the contrary, `std140` has to be used with uniform blocks (a special block that packs uniform variables). The second thing is the condition that prevents out of bounds accesses in our buffers. That could happen because sometimes you could have more work items globally than elements in your buffer. For example, if our buffer has a size of 200 elements, and we use 13 work groups with 16 work items per work group, it makes a total of 208 executions, and our array is sized only to 200 elements. If we don't control those side cases, an error may stop the shader execution, or even worse, crash the application.

As with textures, buffers must be created and managed differently to work with compute shaders (`GL_SHADER_STORAGE_BUFFER`). A new type of vertex buffer target has been added to OpenGL to reflect this.

The following is a host application example of how to execute the previously mentioned compute shader:

```
constintarraySize = 200;
float A[arraySize]; // Input array A
float B[arraySize]; // Input array B
float O[arraySize]; // Output array
// fill with some sample values
for(size_t i = 0; i < arraySize; ++i)
{
  A[i] = (float)i;
  B[i] = arraySize - i - 1.0f;
  O[i] = 10000;
```

```
}
// Create buffers
GLuintinA, inB, out;
glGenBuffers(1, &inA);
glBindBuffer(GL_SHADER_STORAGE_BUFFER, inA); // Bind buffer A
glBufferData(GL_SHADER_STORAGE_BUFFER, arraySize * sizeof(float), A,
GL_STATIC_DRAW); // Fill Buffer data
glGenBuffers(1, &inB);
glBindBuffer(GL_SHADER_STORAGE_BUFFER, inB); // Bind buffer B
glBufferData(GL_SHADER_STORAGE_BUFFER, arraySize * sizeof(float), B,
GL_STATIC_DRAW); // Fill Buffer data
glGenBuffers(1, &out);
glBindBuffer(GL_SHADER_STORAGE_BUFFER, out); // Bind buffer O
glBufferData(GL_SHADER_STORAGE_BUFFER, arraySize * sizeof(float), O,
GL_STATIC_DRAW); // Fill Buffer data
//Bind buffers to fixed binding points (later will be used in the
shader)
glBindBufferBase(GL_SHADER_STORAGE_BUFFER, 0, inA);
glBindBufferBase(GL_SHADER_STORAGE_BUFFER, 1, inB);
glBindBufferBase(GL_SHADER_STORAGE_BUFFER, 2, out);
glUseProgram(computeShaderID); // Bind compute shader
glDispatchCompute(13, 1, 1); // Execute the compute shader with 13
workgroups
glMemoryBarrier(GL_SHADER_IMAGE_ACCESS_BARRIER_BIT | GL_SHADER_
STORAGE_BARRIER_BIT | GL_BUFFER_UPDATE_BARRIER_BIT); // force
completeness before read back data
// Read back the output buffer to check the results
glBindBuffer(GL_SHADER_STORAGE_BUFFER, out); // Bind output buffer
// Obtain a pointer to the output buffer data
float* data = (float*)glMapBuffer(GL_SHADER_STORAGE_BUFFER, GL_READ_
ONLY);
// Copy the data to our CPU located memory buffer
memcpy(&O[0], data, sizeof(float)*arraySize);
// Release the GPU pointer
glUnmapBuffer(GL_SHADER_STORAGE_BUFFER);
// From here, write results to a file, screen or send them back to
memory for further process
```

Summary

In this chapter, we have learnt the basic concepts of compute shaders. As said, they are a complex topic, mainly because of the manual synchronization that must be done to ensure correct results and high performance. We only saw a humble mechanism for that: the `glMemoryBarrier` function which blocks execution until certain operations have finished, but there are many others, even inside the shaders (atomic operations and counters, control barriers, and so on).

It's up to you to discover more about compute shader features such as shared memory access for the work items inside a work group or how to use buffers with complex data structures in conjunction with images to create amazing shaders. You can also learn how to perform pure mathematical functions such as Fast Fourier Transformations or LU/SVD decompositions to make mathematical algorithms two orders of magnitude faster than doing it simply in CPU.

To conclude this book, I would encourage you to start writing your own shaders, slowly at first, assimilating the language's special features, understanding the underlying mechanisms, and coding more and more complex algorithms. With the mechanisms that this book provides, any visual effect that you may have seen in a video game or even in a CG movie can be achieved; so remember, just after finishing the book, start coding!

Index

A

array 28
attributes
    used, in interface blocks 76-78

B

basic lighting theory 50, 51
basic types 19
break statement 25
buffer keyword 93

C

cast types 23
clipping 9
code comments 23
compute shaders 13
conversions 23
crowd of butterflies example 78-84

E

EmitVertex() function 76
EndPrimitive() function 76
examples
    attributes, using in interface blocks 76-78
    interpolated colored mesh 61, 62
    interpolators, using to compute texture
        coordinates 62
    pass-thru shader 75, 76
    Phong lighting 63, 66-68
    solid color mesh 60

execution model
    about 57, 58, 87-89
    fragment shader, terminating 58
external stages 10

F

fill rate 57
fixed design
    and programmable design, difference
        between 10
Flat Shading 51
flow control 23-25
fragment shader
    about 12, 13
    terminating 58
fragment stages 9
functions 29-31

G

geometry sample
    distorting 46, 47
    drawing 44, 45
    interpolators, using 48, 49
geometry shaders
    about 9, 13
    versus vertex shaders 71, 72
geometry stages
    clipping 9
    geometry shader 9
    perspective division 9
    textures 9
    vertex data 8

vertex shader 9
viewport transform 9
glDispatchCompute function 92
gl_Position 43
Gouraud Shading 51
GPU 14, 15
graphics hardware
history 6, 7
Graphics Rendering Pipeline
about 6
external stages 10
fixed and programmable designs, difference
10
fragment stages 9
geometry stages 8

I

input layout
options for 73
inputs 58, 59
input variables 36
instructions 18
interface blocks
about 73-75
attributes, using 76-78
interpolated colored mesh 61, 62
interpolators
about 48
using 48, 49

L

Language basics
array 28
basic types 19
cast types 23
code comments 23
conversions 23
flow control 23-25
functions 29-31
instructions 18
loops 26, 27
matrix operation 22
preprocessor 32-35
structures 27, 28
variable initializers 20, 21
vector operation 22

layout keyword 72
lighting example code 52, 54
loops 26, 27

M

matrix operation 22

N

Normal mapping 52

O

OpenGL
URL 18
OpenGL Shading Language (GLSL) 7
output layer
options for 73
outputs 58, 59
output variables 37

P

pass-thru shader 75, 76
perspective division 9
Phong lighting 63, 66-68
Phong lighting model 50
Phong Shading 51
position attribute 61
preprocessor 32-35
programmable design
and fixed design, difference between 10

R

raw data
computing 92, 93

S

shaders environment 15, 16
shaders types
about 11, 12
compute shaders 13
fragment shaders 12, 13
geometry shaders 13
vertex shaders 12

shader variables
  input variables 36
  output variables 37
  uniform variables 35, 36
Simple lighting
  basic lighting theory 50, 51
  lighting example code 52-54
solid color mesh 60
structures 27, 28

T

texture example
  rendering to 89-92

U

uniform variables 35, 36, 42, 43

V

variable initializers 20, 21
vector operation 22
vertex array object (VAO) 40
vertex attribute
  about 40-42
  examples 40
vertex data 8
Vertex shader input
  uniform variables 42, 43
  vertex attribute 40-42
Vertex shader output 43
vertex shaders
  about 9, 12
  versus geometry shaders 71, 72
viewport transform 9

About Packt Publishing

Packt, pronounced 'packed', published its first book "*Mastering phpMyAdmin for Effective MySQL Management*" in April 2004 and subsequently continued to specialize in publishing highly focused books on specific technologies and solutions.

Our books and publications share the experiences of your fellow IT professionals in adapting and customizing today's systems, applications, and frameworks. Our solution based books give you the knowledge and power to customize the software and technologies you're using to get the job done. Packt books are more specific and less general than the IT books you have seen in the past. Our unique business model allows us to bring you more focused information, giving you more of what you need to know, and less of what you don't.

Packt is a modern, yet unique publishing company, which focuses on producing quality, cutting-edge books for communities of developers, administrators, and newbies alike. For more information, please visit our website: www.packtpub.com.

Writing for Packt

We welcome all inquiries from people who are interested in authoring. Book proposals should be sent to author@packtpub.com. If your book idea is still at an early stage and you would like to discuss it first before writing a formal book proposal, contact us; one of our commissioning editors will get in touch with you.

We're not just looking for published authors; if you have strong technical skills but no writing experience, our experienced editors can help you develop a writing career, or simply get some additional reward for your expertise.

OpenGL Development Cookbook

ISBN: 978-1-84969-504-6   Paperback: 326 pages

Over 40 recipes to help you learn, understand, and implement modern OpenGL in your applications

1. Explores current graphics programming techniques including GPU-based methods from the outlook of modern OpenGL 3.3

2. Includes GPU-based volume rendering algorithms

3. Discover how to employ GPU-based path and ray tracing

OpenGL 4 Shading Language Cookbook, Second Edition

ISBN: 978-1-78216-702-0   Paperback: 398 pages

A full set of recipes demonstrating simple and advanced techniques for producing high-quality, real-time 3D graphics using OpenGL and GLSL 4.x

1. Discover simple and advanced techniques for leveraging modern OpenGL and GLSL

2. Learn how to use the newest features of GLSL including compute shaders, geometry, and tessellation shaders

3. Get to grips with a wide range of techniques for implementing shadows using shadow maps, shadow volumes, and more

Please check **www.PacktPub.com** for information on our titles

OpenGL 4.0 Shading Language Cookbook

ISBN: 978-1-84951-476-7   Paperback: 340 pages

Over 60 highly foucused practical recipes to maximize your use of the OpenGL Shading Language

1. A full set of recipes demonstrating simple and advanced techniques for producing high-quality, real-time 3D graphics using GLSL 4.0

2. How to use the OpenGL Shading Language to implement lighting and shading techniques

3. Use the new features of GLSL 4.0 including tessellation and geometry shaders

Learning Game Physics with Bullet Physics and OpenGL

ISBN: 978-1-78328-187-9   Paperback: 126 pages

Practical 3D physics simulation experience with modern feature-rich graphics and physics APIs

1. Create your own physics simulations and understand the various design concepts of modern games

2. Build a real-time complete game application, implementing 3D graphics and physics entirely from scratch

3. Learn the fundamental and advanced concepts of game programming using step-by-step instructions and examples

Please check **www.PacktPub.com** for information on our titles